250-97

Columbia University

Contributions to Education

Teachers College Series

No. 550

AMS PRESS

NEW YORK

PROBLEMS OF STUDENTS
IN A
GRADUATE SCHOOL OF EDUCATION

BY

DOROTHY C. STRATTON, Ph.D.

144663

TEACHERS COLLEGE, COLUMBIA UNIVERSITY
CONTRIBUTIONS TO EDUCATION, No. 550

Published with the Approval of
Professor Sarah M. Sturtevant, Sponsor

LB1731
S73
1972

BUREAU OF PUBLICATIONS
.Teachers College. Columbia University
NEW YORK CITY
1933

Library of Congress Cataloging in Publication Data

Stratton, Dorothy Constance, 1899–
  Problems of students in a graduate school of
education.

  Reprint of the 1933 ed., issued in series: Teachers
College, Columbia University. Contributions to
education, no. 550.
  Originally presented as the author's thesis, Columbia.
  Bibliography: p.
  1. Graduate students—United States. 2. Personnel
service in higher education—United States. 3. Education—Graduate work. I. Title. II. Series:
Columbia University. Teachers College. Contributions
to education, no. 550.

  LB1731.S73 1972   378.1'94   72-177812
  ISBN 0-404-55550-0

Reprinted by Special Arrangement with Teachers
College Press, New York, New York

From the edition of 1933, New York
First AMS edition published in 1972
Manufactured in the United States

AMS PRESS, INC.
NEW YORK, N. Y.   10003

ACKNOWLEDGMENTS

A study such as the present one cannot be completed without the assistance of many people. I wish to express my gratitude to the members of my committee, Professor Sarah M. Sturtevant, Professor Ruth M. Strang, Professor Milton C. Del Manzo, and Professor Clarence Linton; to the students who participated in the investigation, especially to those who gave generously of their time for an interview; and to the personnel officers and professors who kept the records of their interviews with students.

To Professor Sturtevant, at whose suggestion this study was undertaken and through whose interest it was possible for me to undertake graduate work at Teachers College, I am deeply indebted for wise counsel and guidance. I wish to express my sincere appreciation to Professor Del Manzo, who took an active interest in the investigation from the beginning and to Professor Linton, who made keen criticisms of the study at its inception and throughout its progress. It is a pleasure to acknowledge my great debt to Professor Strang for her generous and untiring assistance in this study and for the inspiration of her creative ideas. Professor Chase Going Woodhouse of the University of North Carolina made valuable suggestions which aided in the definition of the problem.

Finally, I wish to express my gratitude to Mr. Felix Warburg, through whose generosity I was given the opportunity to study at Teachers College.

DOROTHY C. STRATTON

CONTENTS

CHAPTER   PAGE

I. INTRODUCTION 1

Setting of the Problem 1
Plan and Method of the Survey 3
Statement of the Problem 4
Summary of Previous Investigations 6

II. DESCRIPTION OF METHODS 10

Composition of the Student Body 11
The Student Inquiry Blanks 11
The Student Interviews 16
The Daily Schedules 18
Summary 19

III. COMPOSITION OF THE STUDENT BODY 20

Summary 23

IV. AREAS OF PROBLEMS REPORTED BY STUDENTS 24

Personal Problems 24
Academic Problems 32
Summary and Discussion 33

V. SPECIFIC ACADEMIC PROBLEMS 37

The Eleven Academic Problems Most Frequently Reported 41
Summary 55

VI. PROBLEMS OF FINANCE 57

Problems of Finance As Shown in the Student Inquiry Blanks 57
Problems of Finance As Revealed in the Student Interviews 58
Summary 62

VII. PROBLEMS OF PART-TIME WORK 63

Problems of Part-Time Work As Shown in the Student In-
quiry Blanks 63
Problems of Part-Time Work As Indicated in the Student
Interviews 64
Summary 67

CHAPTER   PAGE

VIII. PROBLEMS OF PLACEMENT 69

Problems of Placement As Shown in the Student Inquiry
Blanks 69
Problems of Placement As Shown by Student Interviews . 70
Summary 74

IX. PROBLEMS OF SOCIAL RELATIONSHIPS 76

Problems of Social Relationships As Shown in the Student
Inquiry Blanks 76
Problems of Social Relationships As Shown by Student
Interviews 78
Summary and Discussion 80

X. PROBLEMS OF LEISURE AND RECREATION 82

Problems of Leisure and Recreation As Shown in the Stu-
dent Inquiry Blanks 82
Problems of Leisure and Recreation As Revealed in Student
Interviews 83
Problems of Leisure and Recreation As Revealed in the
Student Time Schedules 86
Summary 97

XI. OTHER PERSONAL PROBLEMS 99

Living Conditions 99
Physical Health 100
Time Distribution 102
Professional Problems 103
Mental Health 104
Home Conditions 105
Religion and Philosophy of Life 106
Adjustment to Physical Environment 107
Personality Problems 108
Miscellaneous Problems 108
Summary 109

XII. THE COMPLEXITY OF PROBLEMS 110

Patterns of Problems in the Student Interview Group . . 110
"Basic" and Associated Problems in the Student Interview
Group 112
Summary 120

XIII. THE PROCESS OF PROBLEM SOLUTION 121

Types of Problems Brought for Consultation to College
Officials 121

CHAPTER   PAGE

Kinds of Assistance Given by College Officials in the Solu-
tion of Student Problems   127
Problems Which Students Attempt to Solve Without Assist-
ance of Personnel Officers and Professors   132
Degree to Which Students' Problems Are Being Solved. .   134
Summary   136

XIV. SUMMARY   138

XV. IMPLICATIONS OF THE PRESENT STUDY TO THE FURTHER DE-
VELOPMENT OF THE PERSONNEL PROGRAM IN A GRADU-
ATE SCHOOL OF EDUCATION   142
Desirable Features of a Guidance Program in a Graduate
School of Education   152

BIBLIOGRAPHY   156

APPENDICES

A. Student Inquiry Blank   161
B. Outline of Interview with Students   162
C. Interview Card Used by Personnel Officers and Professors   167
D. Daily Time Schedule   168

TABLES

NUMBER   PAGE

I. Comparison of Student Body, Questionnaire Group, and
   Interview Group as to Certain Personal Characteristics . . .   15

II. Personal Characteristics of Questionnaire Group and of Inter-
    view Group   15

III. Relative Frequency with Which Personal Problems Are Re-
     ported in the Student Inquiry Blank by 1,000 Students Classified
     by Full-Time and Part-Time Groups   26–27

IV. Relative Frequency with Which Personal Problems Are Re-
    ported in the Student Inquiry Blank by 1,000 Students
    Classified by Women, Men, "Unsigned," Married, and
    Single Groups   28–29

V. Relative Frequency with Which Personal Problems Are Reported in the Student Inquiry Blank by 1,000 Students
   Classified by Age, Period of Study, and Academic Classification 30–31

VI. Relative Frequency with Which Academic Problems Are Re-
    ported by 1,000 Students Classified by Full-Time and Part-Time
    Groups   33

VII. Specific Academic Problems Reported by 1,000 Students . . .   38

VIII. The Eleven Academic Problems Most Frequently Reported
      in the Student Inquiry Blank by 1,000 Students Classified by
      Degree and Full-Time and Part-Time Groups   42–43

IX. The Eleven Academic Problems Most Frequently Reported in
    the Student Inquiry Blank by 1,000 Students Classified by
    Age and Period of Study   44–45

X. Agencies Through Which Students Report That They Have
   Secured Part-Time Work   67

XI. Educational Experience of 126 Students Having Problems of
    Placement   73

XIIA. Average Number of Minutes per Day Devoted to Various Ac-
      tivities by 135 Students During a Five-Day Week   88

XIIB. Average Number of Minutes Devoted to Various Activities on
      Saturday by 135 Students   89

XIIC. Average Number of Minutes Devoted to Various Activities on
      Sunday by 135 Students   90

NUMBER   PAGE

XIII. Average Number of Minutes Spent in Class and Study by 135
Students 92

XIV. Kinds of Leisure Activities Participated in by 135 Students
During One Week 95

XV. Association of Personal Problems in Individuals of the Interview Group 113

XVI. Proportions of Personal Problems Brought for Consultation to
Some Officer of the College 122

XVII. Proportions of Academic Problems Brought for Consultation to
Some Officer of the College 123

XVIII. Frequency with Which Various Types of Student Problems Are
Brought to Personnel Offices 125

XIX. Comparison of Frequency with Which Various Student Problems Are Brought to Personnel Officers as Shown by Students'
Reports and Interview Records of Personnel Officers 126

XX. Degree to Which Personal Problems Reported by 1,000 Students
Have Been Solved 134

XXI. Degree to Which Academic Problems Reported by 1,000 Students Have Been Solved 135

CHARTS

NUMBER   PAGE

I. Activities of 135 Students During a 24-Hour Day, Based on
Records Kept for One Week 87

II. Percentages of Total Leisure Time Devoted to Specific Activities
by 135 Students 96

III. Percentages of Men and of Women Participating in Various
Leisure Activities During One Week 96

Problems of Students
in a
Graduate School of Education

Chapter I

INTRODUCTION

SETTING OF THE PROBLEM

THE present study is one part of a larger piece of research being conducted by an urban graduate school of education for the purpose of ascertaining whether its present personnel program is meeting adequately the needs of its students.

Definition of Personnel Work. Personnel work has been defined in many ways. The Committee on Principles and Functions of the American College Personnel Association defines it as "the systematic bringing to bear on the individual student all those influences, of whatever nature, which will stimulate him and assist him, through his own efforts, to develop in mind, body, and character to the limit of his individual capacity for growth, and helping him to apply his powers so developed most effectively to the work of the world."[1] Hopkins defines it as "work having to do specifically with the individual"[2] and assumes that it does not differ from the concept of education itself. Dean Hawkes of Columbia College limits the scope of personnel work in the following statement: "The time has come for us to take an account of stock of all the work for the individual that is being done outside the classroom, and to make up our minds what is worth doing, how it may be related to classroom work, or what we may wisely omit."[3]

For the purpose of this local survey, personnel work will be interpreted as meaning the extra-classroom services which the college offers to its students.

Lack of Information Regarding Personnel Work in Graduate Institutions. An institution of graduate rank planning a study of its personnel program finds itself severely handicapped both by

[1] R. C. Clothier, "College Principles and Functions," *The Personnel Journal*, X (June, 1931), 10.

[2] L. B. Hopkins, "Personnel Procedure in Education," *The Educational Record*, Supplement, No. 3 (October, 1926), p. 5. Washington: American Council on Education.

[3] Columbia University Annual Reports, *Report of the Dean of Columbia College, 1927*, p. 63. New York, 1928.

lack of guiding principles regarding personnel services which should be given to students in a graduate school and by lack of information regarding the work being done in similar institutions. Although the universities visited by Hopkins[4] in 1925 had graduate schools, his report is confined to the work being done with undergraduates. If graduate students are included, there is no way of distinguishing the services offered them from those given to undergraduates. Again on the undergraduate level, Lloyd-Jones[5] gives a detailed description of the personnel work being done at Northwestern University. This university also has a graduate school, but no mention is made of services being given graduate students which differ from those offered to undergraduates.

Three possible assumptions come to mind to explain the meagerness of written material concerning personnel work on the graduate level:

1. That the same services should be offered to graduates and undergraduates.

2. That graduate students are adults and therefore do not need personnel services.

3. That personnel work with graduate students is a relatively undeveloped field, such services as are being offered having grown up in response to immediate urgent needs and lacking the coordination possible in a program carefully thought out in advance.

Although both groups have some problems in common, such as vocational placement and part-time work, the assumption that exactly the same kinds of services should be offered to students in a graduate school of education as to undergraduate students seems questionable in view of the fact that the students in a graduate school are an older group with the problems of adults. For example, most of them have presumably already made their vocational choices, at least with regard to the general field in which they expect to work.

That the institution making this survey holds the view that graduate students need personnel services is evidenced by its present personnel staff, which consists of a Welfare Director, Physician, Secretary of Student Organizations, Registrar, Secretary to the Committee on Higher Degrees, Social Director and Assistant Social Director in the residence halls for women, Secre-

---

[4] *Op. cit.,* p. 3.
[5] Esther McD. Lloyd-Jones, *Student Personnel Work at Northwestern University.* New York: Harper & Brothers, 1929.

tary of the College, whose office is in charge of admissions, Director of the Bureau of Educational Service and Part-Time Employment, Provost, in charge of loans to students, Business Manager, in charge of housing, and Auditor. In addition to these officers and their assistants, administrative officers and faculty members do a large amount of work with individual students.

The third assumption seems to hold true regarding the personnel work in the institution being studied. Various services have developed as the pressing need of them has become apparent. While each individual office may be performing its duties in a very efficient way, it is difficult to know to what extent the whole organization is functioning effectively in meeting student needs. It is the purpose of the present survey to study this question.

PLAN AND METHOD OF THE SURVEY

The survey comprises two parts, as follows:

Part I. A study of the personnel services which are actually being rendered and of the individuals who are responsible for their performance.

Part II. A study of student problems as stated by the students themselves and as shown by interview records of personnel officers.

The methods used in Part I are similar to those described by Cowley,[6] although developed independently:

1. The head of each personnel office was interviewed for the purpose of obtaining his own picture of his work. This interview was designed to disclose:

a. The phases of his work which the personnel officer considers most important.

b. The changes in his work which he would like to make.

c. The phases of his work which are causing him dissatisfaction or difficulty.

A stenographic report was made of each interview.

2. Daily schedules were kept for at least one week by personnel officers, showing how they actually spent their time. The findings from these schedules supplement the more general information obtained in the interviews.

6 W. H. Cowley, "A Technique for Making a Student Personnel Survey," The Personnel Journal, X (June, 1931), 17-26.

3. Each personnel officer was given a check list of all personnel duties which might be performed in the institution and was asked to check those which he performed alone and those which he performed in cooperation with others. The check lists were used for the purpose of showing:

a. The scope of the work in the institution.

b. The personnel engaged in each phase of the work.

c. The coordination of the present personnel in the performance of each function.

This part of the survey designated as Part I was accomplished by other persons in the institution. The investigation of student problems designated as Part II is the subject of the present study. The statement of the problem in detail and of the methods used in the study will be given in the following sections.

A comparison of the personnel work being done in the college at present with the needs and problems reported by the students should show the points at which the present program meets or fails to meet student needs adequately and should provide a basis for the coordination and development of the personnel work of the future.

STATEMENT OF THE PROBLEM

The present study is as far as the writer has been able to determine the first attempt to investigate the problems of a representative group of students in one institution, in which the majority of the group are graduate students. The aim of this investigation is a fact-finding one. It is an endeavor to ascertain the nature and extent of the problems of students in one graduate school of education. The study approaches, principally from the point of view of the students themselves, the question of the personnel services which should be offered in the graduate school of education under consideration. It endeavors to answer the following:

1. What do the students themselves report as their major personal and academic problems during their period of study in the institution?

2. Are certain problems characteristic of special groups?

3. Which problems are the students bringing for conference to officers of the college? Which officers are being consulted most frequently on the various kinds of problems?

4. Do the students regard these conferences as helpful?

5. How are the problems being solved?

6. What student problems are not being adequately solved at present?

The assumption is not made that it is the function of the college to solve all problems for its students or to remove from their paths as many sources of problems as possible. The point of view is rather that a problem may be a constructive experience, a disintegrating one, or merely a source of annoyance, depending on the nature of the problem and its effect on the student.

The type of problem referred to as a constructive experience may be illustrated by the example of a student who is faced with the problem of choosing between two positions, each offering certain outstanding advantages. The steps involved in making a wise decision on this problem offer an excellent opportunity for constructive thinking. Another example of this type of problem is found in the case of a student who is in doubt as to which of two methods of teaching reading is superior and endeavors to set up a controlled experiment to answer his questions.

An example of a problem which may prove a disintegrating experience is that of a student who is intellectually incapable of meeting the demands of graduate work. His inability to maintain a satisfactory academic record and his consequent failure to obtain a degree may result in loss of confidence in himself, which may have a disintegrating effect in other phases of his life.

The type of problem which is merely a source of annoyance may be illustrated by the case of a student who is forced to waste valuable time waiting in line in the library for books or by one who loses much of the professor's lecture because trucks are unloading coal outside the window.

It is the function of the college to reduce problems of the second and third types to a minimum and to provide in so far as possible an environment which will permit the student to gain experience in solving problems of a constructive kind.

Problems of students may also be classified according to more specific types, such as problems of finance, placement, and social relationships. Within these categories problems differ both in kind and in seriousness. For example, problems in finance range in kind from that of the student who must borrow money in order to remain in college to that of the student who wishes to know how to invest his inheritance; and in seriousness, from the problem of the student who has to borrow two thousand dollars to that of the student who needs only fifty dollars. Between the two extremes of the student who is borrowing heavily and the one who has money to invest is the student who is relying on his parents for support or is living on their savings and has no immediate problem of finance. In the area of social relationships, one individual may have a problem because he lacks friends and associates, another, because he has so many friends he can never call his time his own. Both students have problems of social relationships, but of different kinds.

SUMMARY OF PREVIOUS INVESTIGATIONS

A number of investigations have been made of the problems of undergraduate students. Some have dealt in particular with students who are seriously maladjusted. Such studies do not pertain directly to the subject under consideration, since the present investigation deals with the problems found in a sampling of the entire student group, not with those of a selected group of maladjusted students. Such studies are, therefore, not included in the following summary of previous investigations.

One of the early investigations of the problems of undergraduate students was made by Boraas.[7] He asked all sophomores and selected juniors and seniors in one college to write papers stating freely the difficulties they had experienced as freshmen. All difficulties were listed. This list was then returned to the same students, and they were asked to check the difficulties which they had experienced and to indicate the degree of seriousness by numbering them from one to four. He classified problems into two divisions:

I. Difficulties due to the nature of college life.
II. Difficulties in connection with classes and studies.

The highest three problems in the first division were:

1. Confusion because college life is so different from home life and high school life.
2. Lack of anyone to confide in or take counsel with.
3. Complicated registration system.

[7] Julius Boraas, "Troubles of College Freshmen," *School and Society*, VI (October, 1917), 491-494.

In the second division the highest three were:

1. Selection of studies.
2. No way of knowing how one gets along.
3. Large size of classes. Resulting fear or embarrassment in reciting.

Boraas recommends more guidance in the selection of courses, more consideration to the problem of vocational choice, the elimination of large classes, attention to the deficiencies of the individual student, and a regular program of personal conferences with freshmen.

Bragdon[8] has made a study of counseling problems in five liberal arts colleges for women. She defines counseling problems as "those problems which, for their thorough solution, demand individual consultation between the student and some official representative of the institution."[9] Her study deals with the fields of adjustment giving rise to counseling problems: problems of the prologue to college, of the dormitory, the classroom, extracurricular activities, and individual conferences. She deals also with the personnel of problem solution and makes a critical study of the student interview. From this information she makes specific proposals concerning the organization of a counseling program in a liberal arts college for women.

Angell[10] directed a study at the University of Michigan dealing with the problems of undergraduates in that institution. He studied 216 undergraduates—133 men and 83 women—selected largely from the sophomore class. He secured information relative to the following aspects of adjustment: (*a*) philosophy of life; (*b*) knowledge of own capacities, aims, and interests; (*c*) understanding of life; appreciation of science, art, other social classes; culture; (*d*) self-control, dependability; (*e*) originality, initiative; (*f*) tolerance, scientific thinking; (*g*) adjustment to academic work; (*h*) pecuniary adjustment; (*i*) group relations, social integration; (*j*) congeniality, social facility, tact; (*k*) sex adjustment; (*l*) health.

Each member of the group was given an intelligence test, a

---

[8] Helen D. Bragdon, *Counseling the College Student.* Cambridge: Harvard University Press, 1929.

[9] *Ibid.,* p. 3.

[10] Robert Cooley Angell, *A Study in Undergraduate Adjustment.* Chicago: University of Chicago Press, 1930.

social intelligence test, a fair-mindedness test, and an information test. In addition, each subject had an interview with a psychiatric case-worker and submitted a personal history record. On the basis of the information which he assembled, Angell classified the students as to their academic, social, and life adjustment. He feels that his results are difficult to summarize, but states that his findings indicate the need of a better system of educational advice and of a mental hygiene unit in the college.

Strang[11] studies the personal problems of women students in the freshman and sophomore classes of seven teacher-training institutions. Four sources of information were used: (1) the writings of people in intimate contact with students; (2) the students' own statements of their problems; (3) records kept by deans of all personal problems that came to their attention during one month; (4) schedules of their professional day kept by ten deans.

Seven freshman classes and two sophomore classes were asked to write anonymously the three chief difficulties which they had encountered during their freshman year. Half of the problems reported relate to study. Of these, the most frequently mentioned were difficulty with a particular subject, difficulty with teachers, too long or too indefinite assignments, inefficient methods of work, and difficulty in bridging the gap between high school and college. Social problems constitute one-fourth of the total. Financial problems are common to all institutions.

Green,[12] studying women in two teachers colleges, finds that the outstanding problems are registration, orientation, social contacts, and homesickness.

Sperle[13] studied the difficulties experienced by first year students in teacher-training institutions. She concludes that the outstanding difficulties are:

1. Thoughtless use of time.
2. Lack of skill in using effective aids to work.
3. Reading ability inadequate to meet demands.

The six studies cited above deal with problems of undergradu-

---

[11] Ruth M. Strang, "Personal Problems of Students," *Proceedings of the National Association of Deans of Women*, Washington, D. C., Association, 1929.

[12] Geraldine Green, "Freshman Problems," *Proceedings of the National Association of Deans of Women*, Washington, D. C., Association, 1929.

[13] D. Henryetta Sperle, "Some Difficulties Experienced by First-Year Students in Teacher-Training Institutions," *Teachers College Record*, XXIX (April, 1928), 618-627.

ates. Only one study has been found dealing with the problems of graduate students. Katz and Allport,[14] in their extensive investigation of students' attitudes at Syracuse University, included fifty-six graduate students among those studied. A minor phase of their study deals with the need of advice on personal problems. Students were given a list of items which included general health, nervous or mental troubles, advice concerning sex hygiene, sex knowledge, advice on love and marriage, choice of a vocation, opportunities for self-support, problems of personality, choice of a program of study, change of program of study, methods of study, religion and philosophy of life, and other items, and were asked to check those upon which they had felt the need of advice and failed to obtain helpful advice because they knew of no one to ask or because the advice received was not beneficial. Problems of personality were most frequently reported, being checked by one-fifth of the group. The average number of problems checked by the graduate students was 2.92, as high as the average for any group included in the study.

The present investigation differs from previous studies in the following respects: (1) The field chosen for study; nearly three-fourths of the group studied are graduate students. (2) The differentiation of the problems of various groups of students, e.g., full-time and part-time students, students of different ages, graduate and undergraduate students. (3) The emphasis upon the extent to which problems have been solved. (4) The combination of methods used.

[14] Daniel C. Katz and Floyd H. Allport, *Students' Attitudes.* Syracuse, New York: The Craftsman Press, Incorporated, 1931.

Chapter II

DESCRIPTION OF METHODS

FIVE methods of investigation, listed below, were used in making this study:

1. The official records of the college concerning the composition of the student body were examined to see whether the make-up of the group itself might be such as to give rise to certain personal and academic problems.

2. Student Inquiry Blanks[1] were sent to 3,055 students asking them to state:

   a. The major personal and academic problems which they had faced during their period of study in the institution.

   b. Whether they had consulted anyone officially connected with the college with regard to these problems.

   c. Whether or not the conferences were helpful.

   d. How the problems were solved.

   e. Whether they would be willing to have a thirty-minute interview to discuss ways in which the college might improve its personnel services to students.

3. Interviews were held with 215 students who filled out the Student Inquiry Blanks and indicated their willingness to give time for an interview.[2]

4. Time schedules covering one-week periods were obtained from 145 of the students interviewed.[3]

5. Personnel officers were asked to keep records of all their conferences with students for one week.[4] Professors known to be interested in personal work with students were asked to keep records of all conferences with students not dealing primarily with the subject matter of their courses. All these data were collected near the middle of the winter semester. This seemed a representative period, though certain problems such as those of placement would be more pressing at other times in the academic year.

[1] See Appendix A.　　[2] See Appendix B.　　[3] See Appendix C.　　[4] See Appendix D.

COMPOSITION OF THE STUDENT BODY

The following data concerning the composition of the student body were available from the official records: the total registration of students, the number of men and of women, the number of full-time and of part-time students, the number of graduates and of undergraduates, the age distribution, and the classification of students according to residence.

All data used are for the winter session, 1931-32, with the exception of the classification of students according to residence, which is taken from the Registrar's report to the Dean for 1930-31 and the information regarding age, which is for the academic year 1928-29. It seemed permissible to use the 1930-31 data concerning the residence of students, since the Registrar's records for the past eleven years show little variation from year to year in this respect. In view of the close correspondence existing in the composition of the student body in other respects, as shown by records kept over a period of years, it seemed permissible to use the age study for 1928-29.

THE STUDENT INQUIRY BLANKS

The information concerning the adjustment difficulties which students consider their major problems could be obtained in two ways: through written reports and through interviews with students. Both methods were used in this study.

Use of the Student Inquiry Blanks. The questionnaire method of collecting data has obvious disadvantages. A thorough study of the case for and against the use of the questionnaire has been made by the Research Council of the National Education Association.[5] An effort was made to have the questionnaire used in the present study conform to the suggestions contained in this bulletin.

Katz and Allport[6] state that the validity of information obtained through a questionnaire depends upon the manner in which it meets the following tests: (1) What kind of information is sought? (2) How are the questions worded? (3) How are the results to be interpreted? With regard to the first point, the information requested in the Student Inquiry Blank was within

[5] *Research Bulletin of the National Education Association,* VIII, 1 (January, 1930), Washington, D. C.
[6] *Op. cit.,* p. viii.

the recipient's ability to give and dealt with a subject which concerned students and their welfare. To meet the second test, the wording of the question, ambiguity was guarded against by having students in three classes fill out the questionnaire and write their criticisms of it before it was drafted in final form. The third test, that of the interpretation of the results, depends on the reliability of the answers. The best check of the truth of the statements given in the questionnaires was the interviews with students. The problems mentioned by students who were interviewed were in practically all cases verified as genuine student problems. The 215 students from whom both questionnaire and interview records were obtained reported 457 personal problems in the questionnaires. Of these 457 problems, all but 28 were discussed in the interviews. Of these 28, 2 were not verified because of lack of time; 18 because the problem had been solved at some time previous to the interview, and 3 because the problem was of a very personal nature; in 5 instances no reason was given why the problem reported in the questionnaire was not discussed in the interview. Three hundred twenty-two additional problems were mentioned in the interviews. The fact that additional problems were revealed in the interviews indicates the value of the interview in obtaining more complete information but does not indicate unreliability of the questionnaire used in this study since it asked for the three major personal problems only.

Form of the Student Inquiry Blank. Two forms of questionnaire were considered in devising the Student Inquiry Blank: a check list on which the student would mark the difficulties which he had encountered, and a more informal type in which the student would state in his own words his major problems. The latter type appeared to have certain advantages for this investigation. It gave the opportunity to discover the problems which were outstanding in the student's mind rather than a larger number of problems, some of which might be of less vital importance. It also provided for a more specific statement, and therefore for a better interpretation of the student's individual problems, than the check list would have done. (See form of inquiry blank in Appendix A.)

There was also the question whether the students should be asked to sign the blanks. Since the plan was to interview a considerable number of the students returning the questionnaires, it was necessary to have at least a certain percentage of them signed.

In order to see whether there would be a difference in the type of problems reported by students who were not required to sign their names and students who did give their names, the part requesting the name of the student was crossed out on one of every five of the Student Inquiry Blank.

Selection of Students. Since this study was to be made early in the academic year, it was important to ascertain how many of the students were registered in the college for the first time and how many were former students. If the large majority were new students, the returns might be weighted unduly with problems arising during the first few weeks of school. This information regarding the number of new and of former students was obtained during the registration period.

Each student who had been enrolled previously in the college filled out a card, giving his name, address, major field, degree for which he was working, dates of previous attendance at the college, and number of points carried during each session in which he had been enrolled. The returns showed that 3,483 of the total of 5,664 students registering by October 1 had been enrolled previously. Of this group, 839 had carried 12 or more points during some semester of their study; 195 had carried from 8 to 11 points; 1,773 had never carried more than 7 points; 448 had been enrolled only in summer session or intersession; 228 gave information too indefinite to classify.

The students to whom the Student Inquiry Blanks were sent were selected as follows:

	Number
All students who had carried 12 or more points during any previous semester of residence	839
All students who had carried from 8 to 11 points during any previous semester of residence	195
Students who had never carried more than 7 points during any previous semester	821
Students previously enrolled in summer session or intersession only	250
Students not previously enrolled in the college	950
Total	3,055

The group selected for study contains all students enrolled in the college who had carried 8 points or more in some previous semester and approximately one-half of the other three groups. The selection within each of these three groups was made by choosing every second card from the alphabetically arranged files of students. The selection was made in favor of students who had been enrolled previously in courses giving 8 or more points, because it was felt that the college owes its greatest degree of responsibility to its full-time students and that it was particularly important to ascertain the problems of this group. Moreover, these students should have had more varied contacts within the college than the group of students carrying less than 8 points. There is thus a gradation in the group from students who had previously been enrolled full-time to those whose experience in the college was limited to part-time or summer session work and a still further gradation to those students whose experience in the college was restricted to the first few weeks following registration.

Distribution of the Student Inquiry Blanks. The Student Inquiry Blanks were distributed to students through their major classes wherever possible. Each blank was accompanied by a letter from the Provost requesting the student's cooperation in the study. The weakness of this method of distribution lay in the fact that not all students listing a certain field as their major were taking courses in that field during the current semester and it was therefore difficult to reach them. An effort was made to reach by mail those students who could not be reached through classes.

No effort other than the letter from the Provost which accompanied the blanks was made to secure their return. It was thought better to have returns only from the students who were willing to expend the time and thought required to fill them out than to use follow-up methods to secure a higher percentage of returns.

Return of the Student Inquiry Blanks. One thousand students returned the questionnaires in time for them to be used. The extent to which the replies of the one thousand are representative of the student body as a whole is of course a matter of conjecture. There are two bases for considering them a fair sampling. First, they are representative of the student body in respect to age, sex, and marital status. Second, the relative frequency of each type of problem was approximately the same on the three tabulations made after 265, 580, and 1,000 questionnaires had been returned.

The detailed comparison of the questionnaire group and of the student body is shown in Table I. The classification of students in the questionnaire group is made on the basis of their status in the college. It will be seen that there is a selection within the

TABLE I

COMPARISON OF STUDENT BODY, QUESTIONNAIRE GROUP, AND INTERVIEW
GROUP AS TO CERTAIN PERSONAL CHARACTERISTICS

GROUP	SEX		MARITAL STATUS		ACADEMIC CLASSIFICA-TION		ACADEMIC LOAD		AGE GROUP			
	Men	Women	Married	Single	Graduate	Undergraduate	Full-Time	Part-Time	Under 25	25–34	35–44	45 and Over
Student body Per cent	23.2	76.8	21.4	78.6	63.0	37.0	29.6	70.4	15.2	46.8	28.8	9.2
Questionnaire group Per cent	27.3	72.7	22.4	77.6	72.2	27.8	46.9	53.1	18.6	46.4	27.7	7.3
Interview group Per cent	42.8	57.2	20.0	80.0	82.3	17.7	65.6	34.4	13.0	54.0	27.9	5.1

TABLE II

PERSONAL CHARACTERISTICS OF QUESTIONNAIRE GROUP AND OF INTERVIEW
GROUP

GROUP	SEX*		MARITAL STATUS		ACADEMIC CLASSIFICA-TION		ACADEMIC LOAD		AGE GROUP			
	Men	Women	Married	Single	Graduate	Undergraduate	Full-Time	Part-Time	Under 25	25–34	35–44	45 and Over
Questionnaire group Number	226	599	224	776	722	278	469	531	186	464	277	73
Per cent	27.3	72.7	22.4	77.6	72.2	27.8	46.9	53.1	18.6	46.4	27.7	7.3
Interview group Number	72	143	43	172	177	38	141	74	28	116	60	11
Per cent	42.8	57.2	20.0	80.0	82.3	17.7	65.6	34.4	13.0	54.0	27.9	5.1

*The 175 blanks which were returned unsigned did not indicate sex. Percentages of men and women
are, therefore, based on 855 students.

questionnaire group in favor of full-time students and graduate students. It may be that the larger percentage of full-time students is to be accounted for by the manner in which the group was chosen. It may be that students who have previously been registered as full-time students tend to continue as full-time students.

The somewhat larger percentage of graduate students may be due to a selective factor operating in the return of the questionnaires rather than in the group to which they were sent. Graduate students may feel a greater interest in the college and a greater degree of responsibility to it than undergraduates. From the standpoint of the present study, the selection is desirable in that the investigation is especially concerned with problems of full-time students and of graduate students.

The uniformity of response on repeated samplings of questionnaire returns suggests that, if further samplings had been taken, there would have been no significant change in the relative frequency with which the various types of problems were reported, provided the same selective factors continued to operate.

One hundred thirty-five of the students who returned the questionnaires gave the identification data requested, but did not report any personal or academic problems. This would have been an interesting group to study further to see whether these students really had no problems of importance or whether they were a group who were not disposed to be analytical regarding their problems. They are included wherever the entire group of one thousand are mentioned, but were not studied further.

THE STUDENT INTERVIEWS

Purpose and Plan of the Interviews. The Student Inquiry Blanks were designed to disclose the major areas of student problems, the college officials who were being consulted, and the ways in which the problems were being solved. The interviews furnished the opportunity of investigating the problems more thoroughly.

Bingham and Moore[7] have characterized the interview as "the conversation with a purpose." There were two main purposes in the present interviews. The primary one was to obtain more detailed information concerning students' problems. The second, as has been previously pointed out, was to verify the data in the

[7] Walter V. Bingham and Bruce V. Moore, *How to Interview.* p. 9. New York: Harper & Brothers, 1931.

questionnaires. Three types of information were sought: (1) the factors to which the student attributed his difficulties; (2) the student's method of solving his problems; (3) the adjustments in a specific area made by the student who did not have problems in that area. For example, if the problem were one of finance, was the difficulty due to the student's having come to college without sufficient funds, having found living expenses higher than he had anticipated, or having failed to receive funds he had expected? Was he solving the problem by borrowing money, working part-time, living in cramped quarters, or relying on his family for support? If the student considered that he did not have a problem in the field of finance, was he living on his savings, earning his own way, or relying on his family for support?

In the thirty minutes allowed to the interviewers[8] it was not possible to cover all the areas of problems. It was, therefore, decided to discuss with each student the five personal problems most frequently reported in the Student Inquiry Blanks and additional problems which were peculiar to the individual. In the cases in which additional information was desired regarding the student's academic problems, these problems were discussed also. (See Appendix B for outline of the interview.)

Selection of Students. Those students who were requested to sign the Student Inquiry Blanks were asked also to state whether they would be willing to give thirty minutes of their time for an interview to discuss ways in which the college might improve its personnel services to students, and to indicate hours at which they would be free for an interview. Of the 826 students who signed the questionnaires, 686 indicated their willingness to give time for the interview, 86 did not answer the question, 21 said that they had no helpful suggestions to give, and 33 replied in the negative.

The interview group consisted of 215 students chosen from the 686 who had indicated their willingness to give time for an interview. Two factors operated in the choice of students for the interviews. First, all those selected had reported one or more personal or academic problems. Second, since the interviews were scheduled at thirty-minute intervals throughout the day, it was necessary to choose students whose free time fitted into the schedule. It will be seen from Table II that the personal charac-

---

[8] The writer wishes to acknowledge the assistance of Mrs. Marguerite B. Dubbe, who interviewed forty students.

teristics of this group are in general similar to those of the group of 1,000 students who returned questionnaires. There is a selection in the interview group in favor of men, full-time students, and graduate students.

Technique of the Interviews. Although an outline was used, the interviews were conducted as informally as possible. Some point of interest in the questionnaire was taken as a starting point. As a rule, the students talked freely and seemed glad to give the information requested. Much of the material was obtained from the student's discussion of his problem, without direct question.

THE DAILY SCHEDULES

Time schedules were used to obtain objective evidence regarding some of the problems reported by students. Two hundred five of the students in the interview group were asked to keep time schedules for one week. (See Appendix D for form used.) An endeavor was made to secure their interest and cooperation in keeping the schedules. Many students said they would be glad to know how they were actually spending their time. One hundred forty-five schedules were returned. Ten of these were discarded because they were incomplete or carelessly kept, leaving 135 schedules which were studied.[9]

Students were requested to begin keeping the schedules on the day following the interview. Under this plan the schedules were kept during a series of weekly periods rather than during a single week. Having the schedules kept during different weeks lessened the chances that the returns would be weighted by any one factor, such as mid-semester examinations.

Records of Student Personnel Officers and Professors. The records of the interviews of personnel officers and professors with students were used to obtain a picture of the problems that students were bringing to officials of the college and of the assistance that was being offered students in solving their problems. (See Appendix C for form used.)

Personnel officers were asked to keep for at least one week records of all interviews with students. They were requested to fill out a card for each interview, stating whether the interview was requested by the student, whether he had been referred to the

[9] The writer wishes to acknowledge the assistance of Miss Lois Bennink in this section of the study.

office by someone else, or whether he had come at the request of the office interviewing him. They were also asked to state the specific nature of the problem and the action taken with regard to it. The length of the interview was also requested. Records were kept by thirty persons in the following eight offices: auditor, business manager, educational service, part-time employment, secretary of the college, secretary to the committee on higher degrees, student organizations, welfare director. Important offices from which no records were obtained are: college physician, dean of the college, director of the school of education, director of the school of practical arts, provost, registrar.

Certain professors who were thought to be doing a considerable amount of work with individual students were asked to keep similar records of all interviews with students which did not directly concern the subject matter of the courses they were teaching. Records were obtained from seven professors.

Although not all personnel offices are represented and although the records are inadequate in the length of time during which they were kept, they give a detailed picture of one phase of the personnel work of the college for a short period and they serve as a check on students' reports of the problems which they are bringing to personnel officers.

A total of 859 records of student contacts were obtained from personnel officers, and 88 from professors.

SUMMARY

The method of investigation, in short, was to study the college records of the composition of the student body in order to see whether certain problems might be inherent in the nature of the group itself; to ascertain, by means of the Student Inquiry Blanks, areas of student problems and ways in which these problems were being solved; to investigate through interviews the causes of the problems most frequently reported and the factors associated with them; and to study further through the time schedules specific problems of particular interest. A comparison of the problems reported by students with the problems brought to personnel officers offered a means of discovering student problems which were not being brought to the attention of personnel officers. By the use of these five methods of study a fairly adequate picture should be obtained of problems of students in the college under consideration.

Chapter III

COMPOSITION OF THE STUDENT BODY

PROBLEMS do not arise solely from factors within the individual or from factors in his environment, but from the continuous interaction of hereditary and environmental factors upon the individual. The terms hereditary and environmental are used with the following interpretation:

By *heredity* is meant the influence of factors inherent in the child himself from the time he was conceived. Hereditary influences are intrinsic or innate. Under *environment* is included every influence brought to bear upon the human organism from the time of the beginning of life. The nourishment, the surroundings, the disease germs influencing the child before or after birth, the accidents, education and experiences encountered after birth are covered by the term environment.[1]

Thus the immediate problems of the group of students under consideration are brought about by the interaction between the native and acquired characteristics of the individuals themselves and their present environment. For example, a problem in physical health which may be due primarily to an inherited physical condition may be aggravated by unhealthful living conditions. The disadvantages of an environment which offers restricted opportunities for social contacts may be partially overcome by the individual who has learned to take the initiative in making friends and acquaintances. It is important, therefore, in the interpretation of the problems of students, to consider not only the characteristics of the group reporting them but to consider also certain aspects of their immediate environment.

The location of the college in a large city complicates many types of problems such as finance, transportation, living conditions, health, and recreation. At the same time it offers many opportunities for constructive experience.

[1] Arthur I. Gates, *Psychology for Students of Education*, p. 70. New York: The Macmillan Company, 1931.

Not only is the cost of living higher for students in a large city than for students in many smaller communities, but the opportunities to spend money are much greater. Theaters, concerts, the opera, and the many commercialized forms of recreation invite the student to spend money.

Problems of transportation in a large city include the need of riding in crowded cars, danger from traffic, lack of parking space for cars, and considerable expenditure of time in commuting.

Living in a large city may involve adjustment to noise, soot and smoke, insufficient sunshine, small and poorly ventilated rooms, and lack of space for entertaining guests.

Health problems may be associated with other conditions mentioned. Opportunities for physical recreation may be considerably restricted for the student who is accustomed to such forms of recreation as golf, horseback riding, and walks in the country.

The study of the composition of the student group is of importance both as a potential source of problems and as a basis of interpreting the problems reported. The nature of the student body might be studied from various angles. One might study the social and economic status of the students as Reynolds[2] has done with college students and as Moffett[3] has done with students in teacher-training institutions. One might study the intelligence of the group, their vocational experience, or their scholastic standing. All of this information would be valuable in interpreting the problems of the students. The present study of the composition of the student body deals only with the data which could be secured from the official records of the college. These data are valuable not only as a background for interpreting problems reported by students but also as an indication of potential areas of problems.

The entire student body of the college under consideration numbers approximately 5,600 students, of whom nearly two-thirds are graduate students. The relative proportions of men and women, married and single students, graduates and undergraduates, full-time and part-time students, and students in various age groups are given in Table I on page 15.

[2] O. Edgar Reynolds, *Social and Economic Status of College Students.* Contributions to Education, No. 272. New York: Bureau of Publications, Teachers College, Columbia University, 1927.

[3] M'Ledge Moffett, *The Social Background and Activities of Teachers College Students.* Contributions to Education, No. 375. New York City: Teachers College, Columbia University, 1929.

A study of the information regarding the geographical distribution of the students shows that 68 per cent come from the North Atlantic division of the United States, 5 per cent from the South Atlantic division, 18 per cent from the south and north central divisions, 4 per cent from the western division, and 5 per cent from the insular territories and foreign countries.

The preponderance of women over men, and the wide range in age and in geographical distribution of the student body lead one to surmise that problems of social relationships may be prevalent. Not only do the women outnumber the men three to one, but the social situation is further complicated by the fact that 45 per cent of the men in comparison with 15 per cent of the women are married. Students range in age from under 25 years to over 55 years. Forty-six per cent of the students are between 25 and 34, and 75 per cent are between 25 and 39 years of age. It seems reasonable to assume that the students under 25 and those over 40 will have many social adjustments to make.

The wide geographical distribution found in the student body offers a rare opportunity for students with different backgrounds to become acquainted with one another. It also creates problems in social adjustment which would not be present in a more homogeneous group.

Table I shows also that 70 per cent of the student body are part-time students. For purposes of this study, a full-time student is defined as one carrying 12 points or over, and a part-time student, as one carrying less than 12 points. That this is an arbitrary classification is apparent from the following figures showing the academic load carried by students during the winter session, 1931-32.

	Number	Per Cent
Under 8 points	3,293	58.7
8 to 11 points	655	11.7
12 to 15 points	588	10.5
16 points and over	1,072	19.1
Total	5,608	100.0

Fifty-nine per cent of the students are carrying less than 8 points of academic work. That this situation is not an unusual one is evidenced by the records of the Registrar's office for the past seven years, which show that the percentage of students carrying under 8 points has not been less than 51 or more than 61 at any time during that period. During the past five years it has varied from 55 to 61 per cent. The division between full-time and part-time students is placed at 12 points because that is the distinction generally made in the college.

This classification does not place accurately students who are devoting full time to work for the Doctor's degree but are carrying less than 12 points of academic work. This group constitutes, of course, a relatively small percentage of the student body.

With so large a percentage of part-time students, many problems of conflicts between the demands of academic work and of work for remuneration, and difficulties in planning academic schedules may be expected. The part-time student has special problems of securing the courses he desires at the hours at which he is free to attend classes, of obtaining reference books, of budgeting his time, and of dealing with conflicting demands between his professional and academic work.

SUMMARY

The group of approximately 5,600 students composing the student body represent a wide range in age, geographical distribution, and academic load which they are carrying. Three-fourths of the students are women, three-fourths are between 25 and 39 years of age, three-fourths are single, over two-thirds come from the North Atlantic division of the United States, over two-thirds are part-time students, and nearly two-thirds are graduate students.

The wide variation in age and in geographical distribution and the preponderance of women over men in the student body lead one to surmise that problems of social relationships may be prevalent. The large percentage of part-time students suggests that there may be many conflicts between the demands of academic work and work for remuneration and many difficulties in working out satisfactory academic schedules.

Chapter IV

AREAS OF PROBLEMS REPORTED BY STUDENTS

PROBLEMS reported by students have been divided into the two general categories of personal problems and academic problems. This chapter will consider the kinds of problems classified under each of these two headings, the prevalence of the problems in the total group of 1,000 students and their distribution within various groups.

PERSONAL PROBLEMS

Classification of Problems

The 1,000 students who returned the Student Inquiry Blanks list 1,273 personal problems. These problems have been grouped under the following general headings: finance, leisure and recreation, part-time work, placement, personal and social relationships, living conditions, physical health, time distribution, professional problems, home conditions, religion and philosophy of life, adjustment to physical environment, problems of personality, and miscellaneous problems.

Although most of these classifications are self-explanatory, several may be made clearer by a brief description of the items included under each. Under the heading of personal and social relationships are listed such problems as:

Few opportunities for meeting people.

Lack of normal social life.

Whether to marry now or wait until the financial situation is better.

Time distribution includes problems of the relative importance of academic work and recreation. Mental health problems are largely those of emotional adjustment and worry over questions such as academic standing, finance, the future, possible illness, and securing a position. Professional problems cover a wide range of questions such as:

24

Shall I teach or continue my studies?
Would it be better for me to travel or to go to school?
Shall I do research work or become a teacher?
Shall I continue in my present position or endeavor to secure a better one?

Problems of personality are those of desiring to improve personality and to overcome handicaps such as:

Self-consciousness in a group.
Lack of personal initiative.

Under the classification of adjustment to physical environment are included:

Difficulty of getting used to crowded conditions.
Dislike of city life.
Difficulty of adjusting to life in the city.

Prevalence of Problems

The relative frequency with which problems are mentioned by full-time and part-time students and by the entire group is shown in Table III. Table IV gives the same information under the classifications of sex and marital status. Table V shows the personal problems characteristic of the different age groups, former and new students, and graduates and undergraduates.

Finance ranks at the top of the list for the entire group, being mentioned by 221 students. Next in frequency are problems of leisure and recreation, part-time work, and placement, which are reported 155, 152, and 150 times, respectively. These four problems constitute over one-half (53 per cent) of the total number of problems mentioned. Problems of social relationships are fifth on the list; living conditions, sixth; and physical health, seventh. Time distribution is reported by 7 per cent of the group. Both professional problems and mental health are listed by 5 per cent. Problems in the remaining five classifications—home conditions, religion, adjustment to physical environment, personality difficulties, and miscellaneous problems—make up only 7 per cent of the total number.

Distribution of Problems among Different Groups

The average for the total group of 1,000 is 1.27 problems per person. Full-time students report a slightly higher average of per-

PROBLEMS OF STUDENTS

TABLE

RELATIVE FREQUENCY WITH WHICH PERSONAL PROBLEMS ARE RE-
FIED BY FULL-TIME

| PROBLEM | FULL-TIME STUDENTS | | | | | | | | | | | |
	Women N=283			Men N=98			Unsigned N=88			Total N=469		
	No.	%	Rank	No.	%	Rank	No.	%	Rank	No.	%	Rank
Finance	63	22.2	2	33	33.7	1	25	28.4	2	121	25.8	1
Leisure	64	22.6	1	15	15.3	4	28	31.8	1	107	22.8	2
Part-time work	57	20.0	3	21	21.4	3	9	10.2	6.5	87	18.6	3
Placement	43	15.2	6	26	26.6	2	13	14.8	4	82	17.6	4
Social relationships ..	45	15.9	4.5	14	14.3	5	9	10.2	6.5	68	14.5	5.5
Living conditions	45	15.9	4.5	11	11.2	6	12	13.6	5	68	14.5	5.5
Physical health	28	9.9	8	8	8.2	7	16	18.2	3	52	11.1	7
Time distribution ...	33	11.7	7	5	5.1	9	7	8.0	9	45	9.6	8
Professional problems	5	1.9	12.5	1	1.0	13.5	6	6.8	10	12	2.6	10.5
Mental health	16	5.6	9	7	7.1	8	8	9.1	8	31	6.6	9
Home conditions	3	1.1	14	2	2.4	11	2	2.3	12	7	1.5	14
Religion	7	2.5	10.5	1	1.0	13.5	4	4.5	11	12	2.6	10.5
Miscellaneous	5	1.9	12.5	3	3.1	10	0	0.0	14.5	8	1.7	13
Physical environment	7	2.5	10.5	1	1.0	13.5	1	1.1	13	9	1.9	12
Personality	2	0.7	15	1	1.0	13.5	0	0.0	14.5	3	0.6	15
Total	423			149			140			712		
Average per student .	1.49			1.52			1.60			1.52		

This table should be read: 63 full-time women out of 283 (22.2 per cent) mentioned finance

sonal problems than part-time students, the average for full-time
students being 1.52, and for part-time students, 1.04. The full-
time group which did not sign the Student Inquiry Blanks has the
highest average of any of the groups, listing 1.6 problems per
student.

Men list, on the average, 1.29 problems per student and women,
1.24. Single students report a slightly higher average number of
problems than married students. The average number for single
students is 1.31 and for married, 1.13. Graduates list more (1.35)
than undergraduates (1.13). The highest average number, classified by age, is found in the group between 25 and 34.

Finance is a vital problem to a large percentage of this student
group, if frequency of mention be used as the criterion. Men and
women and both married and single students report finance more
frequently than any other problem. Thirty per cent of the men
list it as a major problem. As will be seen in Tables III, IV, and
V, men mention the problem more frequently than women; full-
time students, more often than part-time; and students from 25

III

PORTED IN THE STUDENT INQUIRY BLANK BY 1,000 STUDENTS CLASSI-
AND PART-TIME GROUPS

| PART-TIME STUDENTS | | | | | | | | | | | | TOTAL | | |
| Women N=316 | | | Men N=128 | | | Unsigned N=87 | | | Total N=531 | | | N=1,000 | | |
No.	%	Rank	No.	%	Rank	No.	%	Rank	No.	%	Rank	No.	%	Rank
42	13.1	2	36	28.1	1	22	25.3	1	100	18.8	1	221	22.1	1
27	8.4	5	13	10.2	4	8	9.2	7	48	9.0	5	155	15.5	2
39	12.2	3	17	13.3	3	9	10.4	5.5	65	12.2	3	152	15.2	3
38	11.9	4	18	14.1	2	12	13.8	2	68	12.8	2	150	15.0	4
45	14.1	1	9	7.0	6	10	11.5	3.5	64	12.0	4	132	13.2	5
24	7.5	6	7	5.5	8	9	10.4	5.5	40	7.5	6.5	108	10.8	6
23	7.2	7.5	10	7.8	5	7	8.0	8	40	7.5	6.5	92	9.2	7
18	5.6	9	8	6.3	7	4	4.6	9	30	5.6	9	75	7.5	8
23	7.2	7.5	4	3.1	12	10	11.5	3.5	37	7.0	8	49	4.9	9.5
12	3.7	11	4	3.1	12	2	2.3	11	18	3.4	11	49	4.9	9.5
13	4.1	10	5	3.9	9.5	2	2.3	11	20	3.8	10	27	2.7	11
3	0.9	14.5	1	0.8	14.5	2	2.3	11	6	1.1	14	18	1.8	12
3	0.9	14.5	5	3.9	9.5	1	1.2	13.5	9	1.7	13	17	1.7	13
4	1.3	13	1	0.8	14.5	0	0.0	15	5	0.9	15	14	1.4	14.5
6	1.9	12	4	3.1	12	1	1.2	13.5	11	2.1	12	14	1.4	14.5
320			142			99			561			1,273		
1.00			1.12			1.14			1.04			1.27		

as a major problem. It ranks second in frequency for this group.

to 34 years of age, more frequently than any other age group. Only 17 per cent of students under 25 report financial difficulties, possibly because many of them are still relying on parental support. The group reporting the smallest percentage of financial problems is the part-time women students.

Within certain groups the problem of *leisure and recreation* is concentrated to a greater extent than finance. Full-time students give it second place in the list of problems; part-time students, fifth place. Full-time women students mention the problem of leisure more frequently than any other problem; part-time women students, however, rank it fifth. The difference between the full-time and part-time students is again apparent in the frequency with which the full-time "unsigned" group and the part-time "unsigned" group report this type of problem. It ranks first for the former and seventh for the latter.

The differences between full-time and part-time students with regard to the problem of leisure and recreation raise the question whether the students spending full-time on study actually have

TABLE

RELATIVE FREQUENCY WITH WHICH PERSONAL PROBLEMS ARE RE-
BY WOMEN, MEN, "UNSIGNED."

PROBLEM	SEX					
	Women N=599			Men N=226		
	No.	%	Rank	No.	%	Rank
Finance	105	17.5	1	69	30.6	1
Leisure	91	15.2	3	28	12.4	4
Part-time work	96	16.0	2	38	16.8	3
Placement	81	13.5	5	44	19.5	2
Social relationships	90	15.0	4	23	10.2	5
Living conditions	69	11.5	6	18	8.0	6.5
Physical health	51	8.5	7.5	18	8.0	6.5
Time distribution	51	8.5	7.5	13	5.7	8
Professional problems	28	4.7	9.5	5	2.2	12.5
Mental health	28	4.7	9.5	11	4.9	9
Home conditions	16	2.7	11	7	3.1	11
Religion	10	1.7	13	2	0.9	14.5
Miscellaneous	8	1.3	14.5	8	3.5	10
Physical environment	11	1.8	12	2	0.9	14.5
Personality	8	1.3	14.5	5	2.2	12.5
Total	743			291		
Average per student	1.24			1.29		

This table should be read: Of 599 women, 105 (17.5 per cent) mentioned finance as a major

less time for leisure and recreation than the part-time students or
whether the part-time students have grown so accustomed to having little time for leisure that they no longer consider it a problem.
Additional data on this question will be presented in Chapter X.

No marked distinction in the prevalence of the problem of
leisure is found between graduates and undergraduates. Sixteen
per cent of the graduates and 14 per cent of the undergraduates
mention this type of problem. It ranks third for both groups.

The percentage of students under 25 years of age listing leisure
and recreation among their problems is smaller than that of any of
the other age groups. Perhaps the youngest students are more
inclined than the older students to take time for recreation regardless of the pressure of academic work.

Part-time work is the problem most often named by the youngest
students and by the new students. The "unsigned" group mention
it less frequently than any of the other groups. One might expect
part-time work to be much more of a problem to the full-time
than to the part-time students. It ranks third for both groups, but

IV

PORTED IN STUDENT INQUIRY BLANK BY 1,000 STUDENTS CLASSIFIED
MARRIED, AND SINGLE GROUPS

	MARITAL STATUS								TOTAL		
Unsigned N=175			Married N=224			Single N=776			N=1,000		
No.	%	Rank	No.	%	Rank	No.	%	Rank	No.	%	Rank
47	26.8	1	51	22.8	1	170	22.0	1	221	22.1	1
36	20.6	2	24	10.7	4	131	17.0	2	155	15.5	2
18	10.3	7	25	11.2	3	127	16.4	3	152	15.2	3
25	14.3	3	33	14.7	2	117	15.1	5	150	15.0	4
19	10.9	6	10	4.5	11	122	15.7	4	132	13.2	5
21	12.0	5	19	8.5	6	89	11.5	6	108	10.8	6
23	13.1	4	21	9.4	5	71	9.0	7	92	9.2	7
11	6.3	9	18	8.0	7	57	7.3	8	75	7.5	8
16	9.1	8	14	6.3	8.5	35	4.5	10	49	4.9	9.5
10	5.7	10	11	4.7	10	38	5.0	9	49	4.9	9.5
4	2.3	12	14	6.3	8.5	13	1.7	12	27	2.7	11
6	3.4	11	1	0.4	15	17	2.2	11	18	1.8	12
1	0.6	14	7	3.1	12	10	1.3	15	17	1.7	13
1	0.6	14	3	1.3	13.5	11	1.4	13.5	14	1.4	14.5
1	0.6	14	3	1.3	13.5	11	1.4	13.5	14	1.4	14.5
239 1.36			254 1.13			1,019 1.31			1,273 1.27		

problem. It ranks 1 in frequency for this group.

is mentioned by 19 per cent of the full-time and 12 per cent of the
part-time students.

Placement is regarded as a major problem by a large percentage
of the youngest and oldest age groups, being mentioned by 21 per
cent of the former and 18 per cent of the latter. It takes second
place with the youngest students and ties with finance for first
place with the oldest group. It is a problem to 20 per cent of the
men and to 14 per cent of the women. It is surprising to find
placement ranking second among problems of part-time students.
One might suppose that the part-time students were already satisfactorily placed in positions. This problem will be considered
again in Chapter VII.

The problem of *social relationships* ranks first in frequency for
part-time women students. It is mentioned by 14 per cent of this
group as compared with 7 per cent of the part-time men students.
Sixteen per cent of the single students state it as one of their
major problems compared to 5 per cent of the married students.
It is fourth in frequency for the former and eleventh for the latter.

TABLE

RELATIVE FREQUENCY WITH WHICH PERSONAL PROBLEMS ARE RE-
BY AGE, PERIOD OF STUDY,

PROBLEM	AGE GROUPS											
	Under 25 N=186			25-34 N=464			35-44 N=277			45 and Over N=73		
	No.	%	Rank	No.	%	Rank	No.	%	Rank	No.	%	Rank
Finance	31	16.7	3.5	125	27.0	1	52	18.8	1	13	17.8	1.5
Leisure	24	12.9	5	82	17.7	2	39	14.1	2	10	13.7	4
Part-time work	42	22.6	1	71	15.3	3	31	11.2	4	8	11.0	6
Placement	39	21.0	2	60	12.9	6	38	13.7	3	13	17.8	1.5
Social relationships ..	31	16.7	3.5	68	14.6	4	23	8.3	7	10	13.7	4
Living conditions	16	8.6	6	61	13.1	5	25	9.0	6	6	8.2	7
Physical health	7	3.8	9	46	9.9	7	29	10.0	5	10	13.7	4
Time distribution ...	14	7.5	7	36	7.8	8	21	7.6	8	4	5.5	8
Professional problems	8	4.3	8	30	6.5	9	10	3.6	10	1	1.4	11.5
Mental health	1	0.5	13.5	26	5.6	10	19	6.9	9	3	4.1	9.5
Home conditions	2	1.1	12	16	3.4	11	9	3.3	11	0	0.0	14
Religion	4	2.1	10.5	4	0.9	15	7	2.5	12	3	4.1	9.5
Miscellaneous	4	2.1	10.5	9	1.9	12.5	4	1.4	14.5	0	0.0	14
Physical environment	0	0.0	15	9	1.9	12.5	5	1.8	13	0	0.0	14
Personality	1	0.5	13.5	8	1.7	14	4	1.4	14.5	1	1.4	11.5
Total	224			651			316			82		
Average per student .	1.20			1.40			1.14			1.12		

This table should be read: Of 169 persons under 25 years of age, 31 (18.3 per cent) mentioned

Living conditions is a major problem to twice as large a percentage of full-time students as it is to part-time students. Sixteen
per cent of the full-time women students in comparison with 11
per cent of full-time men students mention it as a problem.

Physical health is mentioned most frequently by the anonymous
group and particularly by the full-time students in this division,
18 per cent of whom consider it one of their important problems.
It is an increasingly frequent problem in the different age groups,
being mentioned by 4 per cent of the youngest group, 10 per cent
of the next two groups, and 14 per cent of the students over 45.

Time distribution is a major problem to twice as large a percentage of full-time women as of full-time men students. This ranking
is in agreement with their relative placement of the problem of
leisure and recreation.

Professional problems are characteristic especially of the anonymous part-time students. Eleven and one-half per cent of this
group list professional problems in comparison with 5 per cent of
the total group of 1,000 students.

V

PORTED IN STUDENT INQUIRY BLANK BY 1,000 STUDENTS CLASSIFIED
AND ACADEMIC CLASSIFICATION

PERIOD OF STUDY						ACADEMIC CLASSIFICATION						TOTAL		
Former N=709			New N=291			Graduate N=726			Undergraduate N=274			N=1,000		
No.	%	Rank	No.	%	Rank	No.	%	Rank	No.	%	Rank	No.	%	Rank
167	23.1	1	54	19.3	3	154	21.2	1	67	24.4	1	221	22.1	1
99	13.8	3	56	20.0	2	117	16.1	3	38	13.9	3	155	15.5	2
93	12.9	5	59	21.0	1	111	15.3	4	41	15.0	2	152	15.2	3
100	13.8	2	50	18.0	4	126	17.4	2	24	8.8	6	150	15.0	4
94	13.0	4	38	13.6	5	103	14.2	5	29	10.6	4	132	13.2	5
71	9.8	6.5	37	13.3	6	81	11.2	6	27	9.8	5	108	10.8	6
71	9.8	6.5	21	7.5	8	69	9.5	7	23	8.4	7	92	9.2	7
49	6.8	8	26	9.3	7	54	7.5	8	21	7.7	8	75	7.5	8
43	6.0	9	6	2.1	10.5	38	5.2	9	11	1.0	10	49	4.9	9.5
37	5.0	10	12	4.3	9	33	4.5	10	16	5.8	9	49	4.9	9.5
25	3.5	11	2	0.7	15	25	3.4	11	2	0.7	13.5	27	2.7	11
12	1.7	12.5	6	2.2	10.5	12	1.7	13.5	6	2.2	11	18	1.8	12
12	1.7	12.5	5	1.8	12.5	17	2.4	12	0	0.0	15	17	1.7	13
9	1.3	15	5	1.8	12.5	11	1.5	15	3	1.1	12	14	1.4	14.5
10	1.4	14	4	1.4	14	12	1.7	13.5	2	0.7	13.5	14	1.4	14.5
892			381			963			310			1,273		
1.25			1.30			1.35			1.13			1.27		

finance as a major problem.   It ranks 3.5 in frequency for this group.

Mental health is a matter of concern to 7 per cent of full-time
and to 3 per cent of part-time students; to less than 1 per cent of
students under 25, to 6 per cent of those from 25 to 34, to 7 per
cent of those from 35 to 44, and to 4 per cent of those 45 and over.

Problems of *home conditions* are reported more frequently by
part-time than by full-time students; six per cent of married
students and 2 per cent of single students cite difficulties.

Problems of *religion and philosophy of life* are reported most
frequently by the anonymous group, particularly the anonymous
full-time group.   Women indicate problems of this kind more
often than men, and single students more often than married
students.   In the four age groups, students 45 and over cite them
most frequently.

Adjustment to physical environment is mentioned most frequently by full-time women students.

Personality problems are cited more often by men than by
women.   Part-time men students rank highest of all groups in
reporting difficulties in this area.

Miscellaneous problems cover such a wide variety that distinctions within groups with regard to these problems would be meaningless.

ACADEMIC PROBLEMS

Classification of Problems

The group of 1,000 students returning the Student Inquiry Blanks list 1,517 academic problems. These problems have been classified under the following headings: courses, degrees and certificates, study, general advisement, personal and professional development, academic standing, lacks in the physical environment over which the college has control, lacks in training, and miscellaneous problems.

As in the case of personal problems, the classifications of academic problems are arbitrary. For example, problems having to do with difficulty in securing books from the library, which are classed as problems dealing with study, might have been grouped under the heading of lacks in the physical environment over which the college has control.

Prevalence of Problems

An inspection of Table VI shows that 639 students, approximately two-thirds of the group, mention problems pertaining to courses. Over one-third are concerned about degrees and certificates. One hundred eighty-eight report problems of study, and 100 list advisement. These four groups of problems constitute 85 per cent of all academic problems listed. Questions of personal and professional development are cited by 74 students, academic standing by 65, lacks in the physical environment by 39, lacks in training by 29, and miscellaneous problems by 26.

Distribution of Problems among Part-Time
   and Full-time Students

Although part-time students list on the average a slightly smaller number of personal problems per student, the average number of academic problems reported by the two groups is practically the same.

Problems pertaining to courses and academic advisement are equally prevalent among full-time and part-time students, the for-

TABLE VI

RELATIVE FREQUENCY WITH WHICH ACADEMIC PROBLEMS ARE REPORTED
BY 1,000 STUDENTS CLASSIFIED BY FULL-TIME AND PART-TIME GROUPS

PROBLEMS PERTAINING TO	FULL-TIME N=469			PART-TIME N=531			TOTAL N=1,000		
	No.	%	Rank	No.	%	Rank	No.	%	Rank
Courses	300	63.8	1	339	63.8	1	639	63.9	1
Degrees and certificates	140	29.8	2	217	40.8	2	357	35.7	2
Study	75	15.9	3	113	21.2	3	188	18.8	3
General advisement	46	9.8	4	54	10.1	4	100	10.0	4
Personal and professional development	42	8.9	5.5	32	6.0	5	74	7.4	5
Academic standing	42	8.9	5.5	23	4.3	6	65	6.5	6
Lacks in physical environment ..	24	5.1	7	15	2.8	8	39	3.9	7
Lacks in training	19	4.1	8	10	1.9	9	29	2.9	8
Miscellaneous ...	7	1.5	9	19	3.6	7	26	2.6	9
Total	695			822			1,517		
Average per student	1.48			1.55			1.52		

This table should be read: Of 469 full-time persons, 300 (63.8 per cent) reported problems pertaining to courses. This type of problem ranks first in frequency for this group.

mer being mentioned by 64 per cent and the latter by 10 per cent of each group.

Questions of degrees and certificates, however, are reported by 11 per cent more of the part-time than of the full-time students. Study problems are also reported more frequently by the part-time group.

Problems of academic standing, lacks in the physical environment over which the college has control, and lacks in training are cited by approximately twice as large a percentage of full-time as of part-time students.

SUMMARY AND DISCUSSION

This chapter has presented a general view of the types of problems reported by the 1,000 students returning the Student Inquiry Blanks. The following facts regarding the 1,273 personal problems reported appear to be outstanding:

1. Four problems—finance, leisure and recreation, part-time work, and placement—constitute 53 per cent of all those reported.

2. These four, together with social relationships, living conditions, physical health, and time distribution, make up 85 per cent of the total number of problems.

3. All other problems comprise only 15 per cent of the entire list.

4. Finance is the most prevalent of all problems and is common to all groups.

5. Other problems are concentrated to a greater extent within certain groups. For example,

   a. Leisure is cited as a problem more frequently than any other by full-time women students and the full-time anonymous group.

   b. Placement is reported most frequently by men and by the younger students.

   c. Problems of social relationships rank first among part-time women students.

   d. Problems of part-time work are especially characteristic of full-time students, new students, and the students under 25 years of age.

Facts worth noting concerning the 1,517 academic problems mentioned are:

1. Four problems—those pertaining to courses, degrees and certificates, study, and advisement—make up 85 per cent of all problems reported.

2. Problems pertaining to courses alone constitute 42 per cent of all academic problems reported.

3. Full-time and part-time students cite on the average the same number of problems.

The slightly smaller average number of personal problems reported by the part-time students may be due to the fact that the majority of the part-time students are living in an environment familiar to them. Many of the full-time students, on the other hand, have to adjust to new climatic and housing conditions, lack of accustomed facilities for physical recreation, and the requirements of a full program of academic work. They must also find new friends and companions. They are required to make choices between their scholastic obligations and the opportunities which the city offers for recreation and education.

The fact that graduate students in this study report on the average a larger number of problems is further support of the contention made earlier that the need of personnel work is not limited to undergraduates.

The interviews indicate that the high frequency with which finance is mentioned is not largely due to the unusual existing financial conditions, since most students stated that they would have had the same financial problems regardless of the depression. It is to be expected that problems of part-time work and placement should also be high, since they are often associated with financial difficulties. The decreased number of openings in the field of education throughout the country would tend to make the placement problem a serious one for students in the institution studied.

Since financial problems are not mentioned so frequently by the younger students as by the group between 35 and 44 years of age, it may be that the need of part-time work, though frequent among the youngest students, is not so pressing as in the case of some of the older students. The younger students, many of whom are still dependent on their parents for support, may do part-time work because they have an excess of energy and a desire for money to spend on the luxuries rather than the necessities of student life.

The high frequency of problems of social relationships among part-time women students is a matter of interest. The interviews with this group suggest that there are two important factors entering into the situation. The first is that part-time women students who are holding teaching positions and are also carrying academic work have little time to devote to making friends or to attending social affairs. The second is that women teaching in a community in which they have not been reared feel a certain amount of isolation from the life of the adult social group. Their daily contacts are with children, with the exception of their faculty associates, not with the adults of the community, and they often have little opportunity to meet or cultivate people of their own age.

It is to be expected that part-time students, many of whom live at home, would have more problems of adjustment to home conditions than full-time students, many of whom are so remote from their homes that they hear only of the unusual occurrences. The group of part-time students also includes many men who are working toward the Doctor's degree and have left their wives and children at home. This separation naturally causes increased anxiety over home conditions.

It is interesting that apparently students reported their religious and philosophical problems more freely when they did not sign their names to the questionnaire. It seems rather surprising that students over 45 should cite more problems of this kind than the younger students. One might expect students who have reached middle age to have come to some decision regarding problems of this kind.

The problems of mental health have not been emphasized in this investigation because the techniques used are inadequate for a thorough study of mental health problems. Serious cases of maladjustment are not always either recognized or correctly diagnosed by the individual himself. Accordingly, no definite conclusions may be drawn regarding the frequency of mental health problems existing among this group of students.

The large number of problems regarding degrees and certificates reported by part-time students may be due to the fact that it is more difficult for part-time students, limited as they are to certain hours when they can attend class, and continuing their academic work over a number of years, during which requirements for degrees are sometimes changed, to meet requirements for degrees and certificates than it is for full-time students who can concentrate on their courses during several terms. The greater frequency of study problems among part-time students is accounted for in large measure by their difficulties in obtaining reference books.

Chapter V

SPECIFIC ACADEMIC PROBLEMS

THE preceding chapter has shown the general areas of academic problems reported by the 1,000 students who returned the Student Inquiry Blanks. The present chapter will deal in detail with the specific academic problems, with the officials of the college whom students have consulted concerning them, and with the ways in which the problems are being solved.

Table VII indicates the frequency with which specific academic problems are reported by full-time and part-time students and by the entire group. This table includes not only those academic problems which are mentioned frequently by students, but also those reported infrequently. Frequency of mention is only one criterion of the importance of a problem. A problem which is reported by a small number of students may be extremely important to the members of that group.

Forty-two per cent of the 1,517 academic problems reported pertain to *courses*. Eighty-one per cent of all problems pertaining to courses fall under three headings: getting desired courses, choosing courses, and choosing a major.

Two problems constitute 73 per cent of all problems relating to *degrees and certificates*, which constitute 24 per cent of all academic problems. They are problems pertaining to requirements for a degree and the problem of whether to work for a degree. Thirty-five of the 165 students studying for the Doctor's degree report problems concerning the dissertation and 13, problems pertaining to the matriculation examinations.

Problems relating to the use of the library make up 87 per cent of all *study* problems. Other problems relating to study are difficulty in securing the necessary materials for study, which is reported by 15 students, 11 of whom are part-time; and lack of time for study reported by 1 full-time student and 8 part-time students. Problems relating to poor study habits are classified under *lacks in the student's background and training*.

37

TABLE VII

SPECIFIC ACADEMIC PROBLEMS REPORTED BY 1,000 STUDENTS

PROBLEM	FULL-TIME	PART-TIME	TOTAL
Problems Pertaining to Courses			
Getting desired courses	50	137	187
Choice of courses	97	88	185
Choice of major	72	73	145
Covering required work	33	13	46
Courses unsatisfactory	14	6	20
Difficulty with courses	4	5	9
Determining work expected by professors	6	2	8
Specialization within major field	3	5	8
Apportionment of time to each course ...	8	0	8
Extension courses	2	2	4
Indefinite assignments	4	0	4
Getting inspirational courses	2	1	3
Too little opportunity for individual work	1	2	3
Getting stimulating professors	2	0	2
Poor teaching methods	1	1	2
Assistants not well prepared	1	1	2
Limited class discussion	0	1	1
Question whether to drop course for credit	0	1	1
Duplication in courses	0	1	1
Total	300	339	639
Problems Pertaining to Degrees and Certificates			
Requirements for degree	78	73	151
Question whether to work for degree	33	77	110
Dissertation	12	23	35
Evaluation of credits	4	14	18
Matriculation examinations	3	10	13
Take degree in this college or elsewhere. ..	3	7	10
Requirements for state and city certificates	4	5	9
Write essay or take extra course for degree	1	3	4
Hindrance by petty requirements	1	3	4
Which diploma to apply for.	0	2	2
Is a certificate from the college necessary?	1	0	1
Total	140	217	357
Problems Pertaining to Study			
Library	69	94	163
Securing the necessary materials for study	4	11	15
Lack of time for study	1	8	9
How find information in shortest possible time	1	0	1
Total	75	113	188

TABLE VII (*Continued*)

PROBLEM	FULL-TIME	PART-TIME	TOTAL
Problems of General Advisement			
Advisement	46	54	100
Problems Pertaining to Personal and Professional Development			
How heavy schedule to carry	19	13	32
Length of stay in college	12	3	15
Whether to take leave of absence for study	1	3	4
Correlation of courses with daily work ...	2	2	4
Where may I observe good teaching?	0	4	4
Which of two teaching techniques is better	1	2	3
Doubtful about personal qualifications for position	2	0	2
Developing cultural background	0	2	2
How to obtain teaching experience?	1	1	2
Work for grades or for own needs?	0	2	2
How to satisfy entrance requirements in a particular field?	1	0	1
Conflict between work and classes	1	0	1
Difficulty of reconciling differing points of view	1	0	1
Developing a philosophy of education	1	0	1
Total	42	32	74
Problems Pertaining to Academic Standing			
Maintaining satisfactory academic standing	27	19	46
Marking system	13	3	16
How may I find out my academic standing?	2	1	3
Total	42	23	65
Problems Arising from Lacks in Physical Environment over Which the College Has Control			
Physical environment—miscellaneous	12	9	21
Time spent travelling to field work	2	2	4
Getting a place to practice music	4	0	4
Size of classes	2	1	3
Dissatisfaction with seating arrangements in class	1	2	3
Additional equipment needed	2	0	2
Covering distance between classes in ten minutes	1	0	1
Impossible to reach offices before closing time	0	1	1
Total	24	15	39

TABLE VII (*Concluded*)

PROBLEM	FULL-TIME	PART-TIME	TOTAL
Problems Arising from Lacks in the Student's Background and Training			
Poor study habits	12	4	16
Language difficulty	3	5	8
Lack of background in subject matter ...	1	1	2
Competing in classes with older and more experienced people	2	0	2
Lack of familiarity with methods of testing	1	0	1
Total	19	10	29
Miscellaneous			
Registration	2	5	7
Difficulty with professors	0	6	6
Desirable educational outcomes of Children's Tour	1	2	3
Catalogue difficult to interpret	2	1	3
Object to ten-dollar registration fee each session for part-time students	0	2	2
Impatience of clerks in offices	0	2	2
Difficulty of locating people outside of classes	1	0	1
How to make up work after illness?	0	1	1
Lack of cooperation between departments	1	0	1
Total	7	19	26

Problems of *advisement* are of three kinds: those in which the student has felt the need of advisement and has obtained it satisfactorily, those in which he feels the need of advisement but does not know to whom to go to get it, and those in which he has sought advice and either failed to obtain it or obtained advice which has proved unsatisfactory.

Problems of *personal and professional development* are of many different kinds. The most frequently mentioned are those relating to the number of points to be carried and the length of stay in the college.

Sixty-five students cite problems pertaining to *maintaining a satisfactory academic standing*, the marking system in use, and not knowing what their academic standing is. The college under consideration follows the practice of giving students their marks in courses only in summer session and indicating simply "passed" or "failed" in students' record books during the academic year. This practice is followed in the hope that it will lessen the tension and nervousness of students concerning their marks. For some students, however, it creates a problem because they worry about not knowing their academic standing. A number of students expressed anxiety over this matter in the interviews. New students who are accustomed to receiving marks at mid-term and have no idea how they are doing in their major courses and students who are considering working for the Doctor's degree and are uncertain what their marks are reported it.

No one problem stands out from the rest in the group of problems arising from *lacks in the physical environment over which the college has control*. As Table VII shows, this classification covers a variety of different problems.

The most frequently mentioned problem arising from *lacks in the student's background and training* is poor study habits. They constitute a problem to sixteen students, none of them under twenty-five years of age. Students make statements such as these regarding this problem: "Find it hard to concentrate on study after having been in active work for a number of years," "Have never learned how to concentrate," "Have been out of school so long that study is difficult for me."

Miscellaneous problems are of nine different kinds, no one of which is outstanding. It is of interest to note that in a college enrolling over five thousand students a semester, only seven mention problems pertaining to the routine of registration. This apparent satisfaction with the way in which registration is handled is in marked contrast with another institution in which difficulties in registration were mentioned 105 times.[1]

THE ELEVEN ACADEMIC PROBLEMS MOST FREQUENTLY REPORTED

Of the 74 specific academic problems listed in Table VII, four problems constitute 42 per cent: getting desired courses, choice of courses, use of the library, and requirements for a degree. These and seven others—choice of a major, whether to work for a degree, advisement, academic standing, covering required work, dissertation and research, and the number of points to carry—make up 79 per cent of all academic problems. Table VIII shows these eleven problems classified under degree groups and part-time and full-time students; Table IX, under age groups and period of study in the college.

[1] Geraldine Green, *op. cit.*, p. 152.

TABLE

THE ELEVEN ACADEMIC PROBLEMS MOST FREQUENTLY REPORTED IN
AND FULL-TIME AND

PROBLEMS PERTAINING TO	DEGREE					
	B.S. N = 280			M.A. N = 555		
	No.	%	Rank	No.	%	Rank
Getting desired courses	48	17.1	2	123	22.1	1
Choice of courses	34	12.1	4	122	21.9	2
Library	56	19.6	1	82	14.7	4
Requirements for degree	43	15.3	3	86	15.4	3
Choice of major	31	11.0	5	80	14.4	5
Whether to work for degree	16	5.7	8	52	9.3	7
Advisement	29	10.3	6	57	10.3	6
Academic standing	10	3.5	9	29	5.2	8
Covering required work	21	7.5	7	22	3.9	9
Dissertation and research	4	1.4	11	5	0.9	11
How heavy a schedule to carry ...	6	2.1	10	20	3.6	10

* The eleven academic problems listed here represent 79 per cent of all academic problems
This table should be read: Of 280 persons working for the Bachelor's degree, 48 (17 per cent)

Getting Desired Courses. The problem of getting desired
courses is the most frequent of all academic problems. It is
reported by a larger percentage of part-time than of full-time
students, being mentioned by 26 per cent of the part-time
groups and 11 per cent of the full-time group. The preponderance
of this problem among part-time students is to be expected, since
many part-time students hold full-time positions and can devote
only evenings and Saturdays to their college work. The main difficulty of the part-time students is in getting major courses in the
time available to them.

That students 45 years of age and over appear to be more satis-
fied with the courses which they are offered than the younger
students is shown by the fact that 11 per cent of students in the
age group over 45 cite the problem of getting desired courses
while 21 per cent of students from 35 to 44, 18 per cent of those
from 25 to 34, and 20 per cent of those under 25 report it.

The specific problems mentioned under this heading are:

	Number
Courses come at hours when impossible to attend	41
Want specific courses which are not offered	21
Getting courses on Saturday	13
Getting desired courses in the evening	9

VIII

STUDENT INQUIRY BLANK BY 1,000 STUDENTS* CLASSIFIED BY DEGREE PART-TIME GROUPS

FULL-TIME AND PART-TIME									TOTAL		
Ph.D. N=165			Full-Time N=469			Part-Time N=531			N=1,000		
No.	%	Rank	No.	%	Rank	No.	%	Rank	No.	%	Rank
16	9.7	7	50	10.6	5	137	25.8	1	187	18.7	1
29	17.5	3	97	20.6	1	88	16.5	3	185	18.5	2
25	15.1	5	69	14.7	4	94	17.7	2	163	16.3	3
22	13.3	6	78	16.7	2	73	13.7	5.5	151	15.1	4
34	20.7	2	72	15.3	3	73	13.7	5.5	145	14.5	5
42	25.4	1	33	7.0	7.5	77	14.5	4	110	11.0	6
14	8.4	8	46	9.8	6	54	10.1	7	100	10.0	7
7	4.2	9	27	5.7	9	19	3.5	9	46	4.6	8.5
3	1.8	11	33	7.0	7.5	13	2.4	10.5	46	4.6	8.5
26	15.7	4	12	2.5	11	23	4.3	8	35	3.5	10
6	3.6	10	19	4.0	10	13	2.4	10.5	32	3.2	11

mentioned.
mentioned getting courses desired as a major problem. It ranks 2 in frequency for this group

Conflicts in hours at which classes are scheduled	9
Too many theory courses, not enough content	3
Will courses meet my needs?	2
Getting desired courses (specific problem not stated)	89
Total	187

One-half of these 187 students have consulted some official of the college with regard to this academic problem. Of the 110 consultations 99 (90 per cent) have been with professors and 11 (10 per cent) have been with other officials. Students regard 77 per cent of these conferences as helpful and 23 per cent as not helpful.

Students were requested to state in the Student Inquiry Blanks how they were solving their problems. The specific solutions reported were grouped under the following headings: satisfactorily solved, partially solved, unsatisfactorily solved, and unsolved. Those problems for which the students had found no solution are classified under the heading: no solution indicated. In most instances in which a statement is made that a problem is satisfactorily, partially, or unsatisfactorily solved the interpretation is made from the specific solutions stated by the students. The statements concerning the problems which are unsolved are usually those of the students themselves. In reply to the question, "How

TABLE

THE ELEVEN ACADEMIC PROBLEMS MOST FREQUENTLY REPORTED IN
PERIOD

| PROBLEMS PERTAINING TO | AGE GROUPS | | | | | | | | |
| | Under 25 N=186 | | | 25–34 N=464 | | | 35–44 N=277 | | |
	No.	%	Rank	No.	%	Rank	No.	%	Rank
Getting desired courses	38	20.4	3	84	18.1	2	57	20.5	1
Choice of courses	49	26.3	1	90	19.3	1	37	13.3	4
Library	42	22.5	2	64	13.7	4	51	18.4	2
Requirements for degree	34	18.2	4	70	15.0	3	36	12.8	5
Choice of major	25	13.4	5	62	13.3	5	48	17.3	3
Whether to work for degree	14	7.5	7.5	52	11.2	6	33	11.9	6
Advisement	23	12.3	6	43	9.2	7	27	9.7	7
Academic standing	5	2.6	10	24	5.1	8	13	4.6	9.5
Covering required work	8	4.3	9	21	4.5	9	16	5.7	8
Dissertation and research	0	0.0	11	17	3.6	10	13	4.6	9.5
How heavy a schedule to carry ..	14	7.5	7.5	11	2.3	11	6	2.1	11

* The eleven academic problems listed here represent 79 per cent of all academic problems
This table should be read: Of 186 persons under 25 years of age, 38 or 20 per cent mentioned

have you solved the problem?" students often said, "Haven't solved
it," "Still unsolved," "Haven't done anything about it."

The types of solutions reported to the problem of getting desired
courses are:

	Number	Per Cent
Satisfactorily solved	39	21
Partially solved	42	22
Unsatisfactorily solved	16	9
Unsolved	47	25
No solution indicated	42	23

Satisfactory solutions have been reached by:

Studying the catalogue carefully.
Visiting classes.
Being allowed to do extra work for extra credit.

Solutions classed as unsatisfactory are:

Taking courses elsewhere.
Taking courses not wanted.
Giving up courses desired.

One-fourth of the students reporting this problem have not
solved it.

IX

STUDENT INQUIRY BLANK BY 1,000 STUDENTS* CLASSIFIED BY AGE AND
OF STUDY

PERIOD OF STUDY									TOTAL		
45 and Over N=73			Former N=709			New N=291			N=1,000		
No.	%	Rank	No.	%	Rank	No.	%	Rank	No.	%	Rank
8	10.9	5	151	21.2	1	36	12.3	6	187	18.7	1
9	12.3	4	120	16.8	2	65	22.4	1	185	18.5	2
6	8.2	7	119	16.6	3	44	15.1	4	163	16.3	3
11	15.0	1.5	104	14.6	4	47	16.1	3	151	15.1	4
10	13.6	3	97	13.6	5	48	16.4	2	145	14.5	5
11	15.0	1.5	93	13.1	6	17	5.8	8	110	11.0	6
7	9.5	6	61	8.6	7	39	13.4	5	100	10.0	7
4	5.4	9	28	3.9	10	18	6.1	7	46	4.6	8.5
1	1.3	10.5	34	4.7	8	12	4.1	10	46	4.6	8.5
5	6.8	8	33	4.6	9	2	0.6	11	35	3.5	10
1	1.3	10.5	18	2.5	11	14	4.8	9	32	3.2	11

mentioned.
getting courses desired as a major problem.   It ranks 3 in frequency for this group.

In general, full-time students find difficulty in getting courses
desired because of conflicts in the time at which classes are scheduled; part-time students, because of conflicts between their hours
of work and the hours at which classes meet.   Part-time students
often make statements such as this: "There is little to do about
this but to fit in my courses as best I can.   I can't have special
courses to fit my time."   This problem appears to be less capable
of solution by conference than most of the problems included in
this study.

Choice of Courses.   Problems concerning choice of courses rank
second in frequency of all academic problems.   Twenty-one per
cent of full-time students and 17 per cent of part-time students
report problems of this nature.   It is a problem to 22 per cent of
students working for the Master's degree, 18 per cent of students
working for the Doctor's degree, and 12 per cent of those working
for the Bachelor's degree.   As in the matter of getting desired
courses, students under 25 mention problems concerning choice
of courses more frequently than older students; new students
report it more often than students who have been in attendance
at the college before.

The specific problems concerning choice of courses mentioned
are given on the following page:

	Number
Am I taking courses best suited to my needs?	29
Choosing courses within major field	7
Which general courses shall I take?	5
Choosing courses elsewhere to apply here	4
Choosing program in accord with trend of employment demands	3
Choosing courses to help in passing license examinations	2
Choosing courses (specific problem not stated)	135
Total	185

One hundred fifty-five (84 per cent) of the students who mention choice of courses as a problem have consulted some official of the college concerning the matter. One hundred ninety-one conferences are indicated, 183 (96 per cent) of which have been with professors and 8 with other officials. Ninety per cent of the conferences on this problem have been helpful. Regarding these helpful conferences students report: "helpful in suggesting courses which would meet my needs and in some cases allowing substitutes for courses which I did not want, but thought were required"; "considered my previous experience and future plans and helped me work out a suitable program." Types of conferences which were not helpful are: "approved my program without comment," and "professor interested only in one field, not in helping work out a comprehensive program of study."

Students report the problem of choosing courses as being solved as follows:

	Number	Per Cent
Satisfactorily solved	113	61
Partially solved	15	8
Unsatisfactorily solved	14	8
Unsolved	10	5
No solution indicated	33	18

Most students solve this problem after consultation with advisers. Those who do not consult professors solve it by consulting the catalogue and consulting other students. That courses chosen without guidance are not always satisfactory is indicated by students who say that they "chose haphazardly," "don't know to whom to apply for guidance," and are "just muddling through."

Use of the Library. Problems relating to the library rank third in frequency and are characteristic of all groups. The following kinds of problems are listed under this heading:

	Number
Difficulty in learning how to use the library	39
Difficulty in getting reference books	34
Difficulty in getting material desired	33
Difficulty in getting books for home use	13
Time lost looking for books	12
Time lost waiting for books	7
Difficulties due to crowded conditions	5
Lack of materials in specific fields	5
Difficulty in obtaining part-time student's card	5
Books listed in card files missing	3
Irritating restrictions	2
Obtaining permission to use other libraries	1
Time lost owing to wrong information	1
No Sunday papers available	1
Difficulty in the use of card files	1
Librarians uninterested in giving information	1
Total	163

Thirty-five per cent of the students who list problems in connection with the library have consulted some official of the college concerning their difficulties, 65 per cent have not. Eighty-three per cent of those consulted are librarians; 17 per cent are professors. Students report only 51 per cent of these conferences as having been helpful. The following figures give the stages of solution in which students report their library problems:

	Number	Per Cent
Satisfactorily solved	24	15
Partially solved	10	6
Unsatisfactorily solved	38	23
Unsolved	39	24
No solution indicated	52	32

A small percentage of students have been able to solve their library problems satisfactorily. Those who report difficulty in learning how to use the library have been helped by having librarians explain to them how to find books. Solutions to library problems regarded as unsatisfactory are "buy books," "use other libraries," and "do without material."

Degree Requirements. One hundred fifty-one students report determining requirements for a degree as a problem. Specific problems are of the following kinds:

	Number
Desired and required courses at variance	24
Meeting requirements within specified time limit	4
Meeting requirements by essay or extra points	3
Difficulty in securing courses to meet requirements	2
Reconciling degree requirements with personal and professional needs	2
Meeting requirements without narrowing field of study too greatly	2
Not enough required courses from which to choose	1
How complete requirements by taking evening courses?	1
Determining requirements for diploma	1
Catalogue lacking in information regarding requirements	1
Meeting residence requirements	1
No credit recognition of teaching experience	1
Determining requirements for a degree (specific problem not stated)	108
Total	151

One hundred nine students report 146 conferences with officers of the college regarding the matter of meeting the requirements for a degree. Professors have been consulted 104 times and other officials 42 times, the latter including Secretary of the College, 19 times; Secretary to Committee on Higher Degrees, 11; Director of School of Education, 4; Director of School of Practical Arts, 2. Eighty-four per cent of these conferences were reported to have been helpful and 16 per cent were not so considered. As is shown in the list above, the most common problem is that of determining what the requirements for the degree are and in working out a program to meet them. Almost all conferences were on this phase of the problem and consisted in securing an explanation of requirements to be met. Solutions reported by students may be classified as follows:

	Number	Per Cent
Satisfactorily solved	60	40
Partially solved	12	8
Unsatisfactorily solved	15	10
Unsolved	34	22
No solution indicated	30	20

Unsatisfactory solutions reported are "delay in securing degree due to not having met requirements," and "taking extra points to meet requirements."

Choice of a Major. Choosing a major has been a problem to 145 students. Although reported by all groups, candidates for the Doctor's degree mention it more frequently than any other group. Only three kinds of problems are listed under this heading:

	Number
Choice of major	109
Change of major	29
Have I chosen best major for myself?	7
Total	145

Seventy-five per cent of the students have conferred with college officials concerning this problem. A total of 177 conferences are reported. Ninety per cent of the conferences have been with professors and 10 per cent have been with other officials. The Secretary of the College is named by eleven students as one of the officials consulted. Eighty-eight per cent of the conferences are regarded as helpful; 12 per cent are not. Students report solutions to the problem as follows:

	Number	Per Cent
Satisfactorily solved	87	60
Partially solved	12	8
Unsatisfactorily solved	6	4
Unsolved	23	16
No solution indicated	17	12

This problem is one of the most vital in the entire list of academic problems. It not only involves the work the student will take while in the college, but will probably influence the kind of position he will secure after leaving school. In view of this fact, it is unfortunate that 58 of the 145 students who cite this problem find themselves still uncertain whether they have chosen wisely. Mature students should not be floundering in their work as is this man: "By accident, I just started in my present major and I still happen to be there. As a matter of fact, I am still undecided as to the best major for myself." One woman studying for the Master's degree states, "I consulted the advisers during registration concerning the choice of a major with a view to future vocational placement, but received no helpful suggestions. I had to change my major in the middle of the year after I had felt around and found my main interest." Another says, "My adviser has no apparent interest in my individual needs and aims."

Ways in which conferences on this problem were considered helpful are: "helpful, in that the future in various lines of work was indicated"; "explained the field to me, and I found out it was not what I wanted"; "explained the content of the courses to me." Those students whose conferences were unsatisfactory state that "extra courses and time are required to complete work," "am attempting my own solution after unsatisfactory conference," and "because of conflicting advice I chose a different major."

Whether to Work for a Degree. The question of whether to work for a degree is reported most frequently by students working for the Doctor's degree. Twenty-five per cent of this group list this problem in comparison with 11 per cent of the entire group. Problems mentioned are:

	Number
Shall I work for a degree?	96
Am I too old to work for a degree?	4
Is a higher degree worth the time and money required?	3
Shall I work for a degree or take the courses I want?	2
Is a Doctor's degree worth while for a woman?	1
Shall I work for the Doctor's degree now or get experience first?	1
Can I earn a degree in five years on part-time?	1
Shall I work for a degree and keep my teaching position?	1
What degree shall I work for?	1
Total	110

Sixty-five per cent of the 110 students listing this problem have consulted some college official regarding it. Of the 112 conferences reported, 88 per cent were with professors and 12 per cent were with other officials. The Director of the School of Education is mentioned seven times as one of the officials consulted. Ninety-two per cent of the conferences on this problem are helpful. Students are solving it as follows:

	Number	Per Cent
Satisfactorily solved	54	49
Partially solved	5	4
Unsatisfactorily solved	1	1
Unsolved	36	33
No solution indicated	14	13

Advisement. Although problems of advisement are given a separate heading, they by no means comprise all problems on which students feel the need of advice. For example, questions involving choice of courses, choice of major, and decision as to whether to work for a degree, are essentially counseling problems.

One hundred students state in the Student Inquiry Blanks that advisement is a major problem to them.

New students and those under 25 list problems of advisement more frequently than any other group. The following statement made by a man working for the Master's degree is illustrative of the problems reported: "My most vital problem has been that of obtaining intimate and interested advisement. Coming from a small college I missed the close contact enjoyed by the student with his adviser. I have been merely one of the crowd. The bigger the classes, the more popular, and apparently the more successful, the instructor. I oftentimes feel that I am just one of the insignificant members of a large commercialized educational system."

Specific problems under this heading are:

	Number
Advisement	49
Advice regarding subjects	20
Lack of adequate advisement	8
Difficulty in obtaining advice	6
Advice during registration too hurried	5
Uncertain whom to see for advice	4
Getting an adviser	4
Loss of credit through poor advice	2
Advice needed concerning choice of major	2
Total	100

Seventy-two per cent have conferred with college authorities concerning their problem. Eighty-one conferences are reported. Ninety per cent of the officers consulted were professors; 10 per cent were other officials of the college. Sixty-eight per cent of the students consider these conferences helpful, 32 per cent do not consider them helpful. The state of solutions reported is as follows:

	Number	Per Cent
Satisfactorily solved	28	28
Partially solved	16	16
Unsatisfactorily solved	9	9
Unsolved	24	24
No solution indicated	23	23

That students consider the matter of obtaining advisement on academic problems a major problem is shown clearly by statements made in the student interviews. When asked whether they had any suggestions concerning the ways in which the college might improve its personnel services to students, the suggestions most frequently made by students was that they would appreciate more opportunities for conferences with professors. Statements such as the following were made a number of times:

Students feel professors lack time to give attention to student problems. Students are extremely conscious of the fact that professors are rushed. Could we have a professor assigned to small groups of students so that we could feel free to go to him?

I wish instructors could have more time to answer students' questions. Students feel they are robbing professors of their time to go to their offices.

I feel the need of an academic adviser, someone interested in me. I have never felt anyone was particularly interested.

Students need more adequate advice on dissertation problems. They sometimes work for several months and find there is really no problem.

I should like to be advised as to what openings there are in various educational fields.

I feel the need of an academic adviser who is not connected with any department.

I seriously needed advice regarding courses when I first came. I came directly from college and planned to take two years for my Master's degree. I wanted my courses to contribute to growth, not be merely additions. I feel I have wasted considerable time.

An analysis of students' reports suggests the following weaknesses in academic advisement:

a. Lack of guidance in courses due to:
1) Advisers not available or too hurried.
2) Uncertainty as to the proper person to see.
3) Lack of knowledge of state requirements on the part of advisers.
4) Lack of agreement on requirements among advisers.
5) Lack of knowledge of student's background by adviser.
6) Lack of knowledge of content of courses.
7) Faulty line of reference (passed from one person to another).
8) Advisers' bias in favor of certain courses.

b. Lack of guidance in regard to professional field:
  1) Choice between position and further study.
  2) Choice of field of work.
  3) Opportunities in various educational fields.
c. Lack of interest in the student as an individual.
d. Lack of guidance in research:
  1) Choice of dissertation problem.
  2) Development of dissertation problem.
  3) Independent problems.

Academic Standing. The matter of academic standing has been mentioned earlier in this chapter. Only 15 students (23 per cent) report consultations with any college official concerning this problem. Of 18 officers consulted, 17 were professors. Seventy-two per cent of the conferences were reported as helpful; 28 per cent as not. The state of solutions reported is as follows:

	Number	Per Cent
Satisfactorily solved	8	12
Partially solved	15	23
Unsatisfactorily solved	5	8
Unsolved	22	34
No solution indicated	15	23

Covering Required Work. Covering required work presents a difficulty to 46 students. Only 7 of the 46 have consulted with professors or other officials concerning the matter. Six of the 7 consultations were with professors. Three were helpful and 4 were not. Specific problems reported are:

	Number
Difficulty in covering amount of work required	17
Reading lists too heavy	15
Difficulty in securing books for outside reading	4
Too many papers required	3
Difficulty in covering work while teaching	3
Most efficient way to do required work without injuring health	3
One course requires too much time	1
Total	46

It is of interest that 46 students cite problems pertaining to doing the amount of work required and only 9 report problems of difficulty in mastering the subject matter of the courses. This emphasis upon covering the work required raises the question whether certain professors are requiring too large a quantity of work possibly at the expense of quality. Information concerning the amount of time students are actually spending in preparation for their courses, as shown by daily time schedules, will be given in Chapter X.

The solution most commonly reported to this problem is "have learned to skim readings quickly."

Dissertation and Research. Problems regarding dissertation and research are cited by 35 students. They are of the following kinds:

	Number
Formulating a problem for a dissertation	17
Securing guidance in research	10
Can I afford time and money for a dissertation?	3
Financing dissertation	2
Choosing a sponsor and committee	1
Arranging schedule to allow time for dissertation	1
Getting thesis approved	1
Total	35

Thirty-four of these 35 students have had conferences regarding their research problems. Of the 53 conferences reported, 49 were with professors, 3 were with the Director of the School of Education, and one was with the Director of the School of Practical Arts. Thirty-nine conferences were reported as helpful; 11 as not.

The state of solutions reported is as follows:

	Number	Per Cent
Satisfactorily solved	5	14
Partially solved	1	3
Unsolved	24	69
No solution indicated	5	14

How Heavy a Schedule to Carry. Nineteen of the 32 students who mention the problem of how heavy a schedule to carry have consulted professors concerning the matter. No other official is mentioned as a consultant. All conferences are reported as helpful. Specific problems of this nature are:

	Number
How many points shall I carry?	17
Working part-time, how many points shall I take?	9
Physically below par, how much work shall I carry?	3
Have been out of school several years; shall I carry full schedule?	2

Shall I spread work over several years or try to
complete it in one year?   I
     Total   32

This is the only academic problem which shows a perfect record of
helpful conferences. The state of solutions reported is as follows:

	Number	Per Cent
Satisfactorily solved	20	62
Partially solved	4	13
Unsatisfactorily solved	I	3
Unsolved	2	6
No solution indicated	5	16

SUMMARY

Eleven problems constitute 1,200 of the 1,517 academic problems reported. They are those of getting desired courses, choosing courses, use of the library, requirements for a degree, choice
of a major, decision as to whether to work for a degree, advisement, academic standing, covering required work, dissertation and
research, and the number of points to carry. Sixty-one per cent
of these problems have been brought to some college officer for
conference. The very large part played by the faculty in counseling on academic problems is indicated by the fact that 815 (84 per
cent) of the 967 conferences reported have been with professors.
Eighty-two per cent of the conferences are considered helpful.

One reason for the relatively small number of conferences with
officials of the college other than faculty members may be the fact
that students do not know to whom to go to obtain assistance in
the solution of certain problems. For example, some students
may not know that there are assistants in the Office of the Secretary who can help them in the solution of many of their major
academic problems.

Perhaps the outstanding fact regarding the academic problems
is that nearly all are of the kind that can be solved, or at least
set on the road to solution, by conferences with college officers.
With the exception of the problems of part-time students who
cannot get courses desired because their work for remuneration
takes all their time except the evening hours, the eleven problems
most frequently reported all appear to be soluble by conference.

Many of these problems are of the kind described earlier as constructive. For example, the fact that many students list choosing

courses and choosing a major as important academic problems indicates that they think about these matters. The most important
point to be considered is whether or not they have been able to
solve their problems satisfactorily. The following tabulation shows
that slightly over a third of the eleven problems most frequently
reported have been satisfactorily solved.

	Number	Per Cent
Satisfactorily solved	441	37
Partially solved	146	12
Unsatisfactorily solved	109	9
Unsolved	264	22
No solution indicated	240	20

One of the outstanding findings of the interviews was the fact
that students frequently reported the need of academic advisement.
Many students stated that their major academic difficulty had been
that of obtaining adequate educational guidance and expressed the
desire to have some one professor whom they could consider their
adviser.

Chapter VI

PROBLEMS OF FINANCE

Prevalence and Kinds of Problems. As stated in Chapter IV, finance is the most prevalent of all personal problems, being reported by 221 students. It is of frequent occurrence with all age groups, part-time and full-time students, men and women, new and former students, married and single students, and those working for all degrees.

Financial problems appear to differ more in acuteness than in kind. Of the total number of specific financial problems mentioned, only 3 deal with questions not directly pertaining to lack of funds. One is a problem of where to deposit money and 2 are problems of investing savings. Specific financial problems reported are:

	Number
Where can I get money to continue my education?	12
Where can I get money to pay tuition?	10
How shall I budget my money to cover expenses?	5
Finds expected funds are not available	5
Shall I borrow money to continue school or stop and teach?	3
Shall I borrow money or work part-time?	2
How to invest savings	2
How can I repay money borrowed last year?	1
How can I help support my parents and continue in school?	1
Catalogue budget too small	1
Shall I go in debt for an education at middle age?	1
Where can I get money to finance my dissertation?	1
Finance (specific problem not stated)	177
Total	221

Consultation Regarding Problems. Eighty (36 per cent) of the students reporting financial problems have consulted college officials concerning them. One hundred three conferences are reported with the following officials:

42 with professors
17 with the Provost
17 with other officials of the college
9 with the Bureau of Part-time Employment
6 with the Secretary of the College
6 with the Bursar
6 with the Welfare Director

Students consider 87 per cent of these conferences helpful and consider 13 per cent of no help.

Degree to Which Problems Have Been Solved. Students report their financial problems solved to the following degree:

	Number	Per Cent
Satisfactorily solved	105	47.5
Partially solved	26	11.8
Unsatisfactorily solved	8	3.6
Unsolved	53	24.0
No solution indicated	29	13.1

The 105 students who have solved their financial problems satisfactorily have done so in the following ways:

48 are borrowing money
37 have part-time work
12 have scholarships
4 are paying tuition on the installment plan
3 have fellowships
1 deposits money in student bank

PROBLEMS OF FINANCE AS REVEALED IN STUDENT INTERVIEWS

Considering the prevalence of financial problems, the following questions come to mind:

1. What are the immediate causes underlying the students' financial problems? Have the problems arisen because of loss of position, failure to obtain money which had been anticipated, failure to obtain part-time work, or other factors?

2. How did the students plan to solve their financial problems?

3. How are they solving them?

4. What percentage of students are dependent in whole or in part on their own resources? What percentage are responsible for the support of others?

5. To what extent is the prevalence of financial problems a result of the current financial depression?

6. How are those students who do not report financial problems meeting their financial obligations?

The student interviews were planned to investigate these questions.

Causes of Financial Problems. One hundred twenty-five of the 215 students interviewed have financial problems. The causes of their problems, as stated by 107 of the 125, are as follows:

> 23 had insufficient funds when they came to school
> 18 have been unable to obtain full-time or part-time work
> 13 have lost their positions
> 10 are supporting others
> 8 have lost money in bank failures
> 7 have remained in school longer than they had intended
> 6 have found living costs higher than anticipated
> 5 have had unexpected expenses
> 5 are hampered by reduced incomes
> 4 have poor health
> 4 have found their funds unavailable
> 2 are just out of college
> 1 has lost money through a fall in the rate of exchange
> 1 is paying back borrowed money

Ways in Which Students Planned to Solve Their Problems and Ways in Which They Are Solving Them. Fifty-two per cent of students with financial problems planned to solve them by full-time or part-time work and 37 per cent planned to solve them by borrowing money. The remaining 11 per cent expected to sell property or live on their savings. The ways in which they actually are solving them, as stated by 100 students, are as follows:

> 61 are borrowing money
> 22 are working part-time
> 7 are living on their resources and are expecting to borrow later
> 4 have not solved them
> 4 are working full-time
> 1 is paying tuition in monthly installments
> 1 is using money from the sale of property

One decided difference is apparent between the ways in which the students planned to meet their financial problems and the ways in which they actually are meeting them. More students are borrowing money and fewer are working either part-time or full-time than originally planned to do so. Thirty-seven per cent of the students planned to borrow; 61 per cent are borrowing. Fifty-two per cent planned to work full-time or part-time; 26 per cent are doing so.

Most of the students turn to relatives and friends for financial assistance. Of the 61 students who are borrowing, 41 are drawing from these sources. Twenty-four are borrowing from both relatives and friends; 13, from relatives alone; and 4, from friends alone. Ten are borrowing from the college, 7 are borrowing on their insurance policies, and only 3 are borrowing from banks. Five students who are in the "no problem" group financially are borrowing money, but feel that they have assets to offset the debts. Some state that they may have to borrow additional money before the close of the academic year. The amounts borrowed are:

3 are borrowing $2,000 and over
2 are borrowing $1,500 to $1,999
7 are borrowing $1,000 to $1,499
24 are borrowing $500 to $999
15 are borrowing $250 to $499
10 are borrowing under $250

Thirty-eight per cent of the group pay no interest; 28 per cent pay 2 per cent interest, the amount charged on loans by the college; 7 per cent 3, 4, and 5 per cent interest; 22 per cent pay 6 per cent; and 5 per cent pay 7 and 8 per cent interest.

Eight of the 215 students hold fellowships, 4 of which are from the college and 4 from other sources. Twenty-one have scholarships, 12 of which are from the college and 9 from other sources. The amounts of the 8 fellowships vary as follows:

4 are $1,500 and over
2 are $1,000 to $1,499
1 is from $500 to $750
1 is less than $500

The 21 scholarships are for the following amounts:

10 are $500 or over
6 are $250 to $499
3 cover tuition
2 are less than $250

Students Dependent on Their Own Resources. One hundred thirty of the 170 students from whom the information was obtained are dependent entirely on their own resources, 33 are partially dependent on their own resources, and 7 are dependent entirely on other sources for support.

Students Who Aid in the Support of Others. Not only do most of the group rely on their own resources, but many aid in the support of others. One hundred seventy-three gave definite information on this question. Of this number, 28 men and 31 women have the following relatives depending upon them in whole or in part for support:

	Number
One Dependent	
Mother	16
Wife	9
Sister or brother	6
Child	2
Total	33
Two Dependents	
Wife and child	6
Father and mother	6
Mother and sister	2
Father and sister	1
Wife and brother	1
Total	16
Three Dependents	
Wife and 2 children	3
Father, mother, and child	2
Father, wife, and sister	1
Father, mother, and sister	1
Total	7
Four Dependents	
Wife and 3 children	1
Father, mother, brother, and sister	1
Total	2
Five Dependents	
Wife and 4 children	1
Total	1

Influence of Financial Depression on Prevalence of Problems. From 107 of the 125 students who consider that they have financial problems information was obtained as to the influence of the current financial depression upon their financial difficulties. Sixty-seven state that they would have had financial problems regardless of the depression, for 25 the problem would not have been so acute, and 15 state that they would not have had financial problems if the general financial situation had been normal.

Students Not Having Financial Problems. Ninety students (42 per cent) state that finance is not a problem to them. From 69 of this group of 90 the following information was obtained as to how they are meeting their financial obligations:

21 are living on their savings
19 are doing full-time work
7 are doing part-time work
7 are relying on their families in whole or in part for support
7 have independent incomes
6 are on leave of absence with income
2 have scholarships or fellowships

SUMMARY

The Student Inquiry Blanks indicate that:

1. Finance is the most prevalent of all personal problems, being mentioned frequently by all groups.

2. Slightly less than one-half of the students have been able to solve their financial problems satisfactorily.

Interviews with students show that:

1. Over one-fourth of the financial problems have arisen because students have been unable to work full time or part time.

2. More students are borrowing money and fewer are working part-time than originally planned to do so.

3. Two-thirds of the students who are borrowing are obtaining money from relatives and friends. Only 5 per cent are borrowing from banks. Four-fifths are borrowing less than $1,000. The amounts most frequently borrowed are in the $500 to $999 interval.

4. Approximately one-seventh of the entire group interviewed have fellowships or scholarships which aid in meeting their expenses.

5. Over three-fourths are dependent entirely on their own resources.

6. One-third of the group aid in the support of one or more relatives.

7. One-seventh of the students with financial problems attribute their difficulties directly to the depression. One-fourth more state that their problems would not have been so acute under normal conditions.

8. Over one-third of the students who do not report financial problems are working full time or part time.

Chapter VII

PROBLEMS OF PART-TIME WORK

CLOSELY related to problems of finance are problems of part-time work. Few students in a professional school would deliberately choose to spend time in employment not directly connected with their academic work unless forced to do so to meet expenses. If these problems are considered as one aspect of financial problems, the spread of financial difficulties becomes even greater than is shown by the number of financial problems reported.

The present chapter will deal with the kinds of part-time work being done by students, the wages which they receive for their work, the agencies through which they secure employment, and their estimates of the value of their part-time work to their professional advancement.

PROBLEMS OF PART-TIME WORK AS SHOWN IN THE STUDENT
INQUIRY BLANKS

Prevalence and Kinds of Problems. One hundred fifty-two students report problems of part-time work. The specific problems and their frequency are as follows:

	Number
Obtaining part-time work	110
Shall I carry full schedule or work part-time?	36
Obtaining part-time work for the summer	3
Difficulty in doing part-time work and getting courses desired	2
Conflict between part-time work and study	1

Consultations Concerning Problems. Sixty-seven per cent of these 152 students report that they have conferred with some officer of the college regarding these problems. Fifty per cent of the conferences were with the staff of the Bureau of Part-Time Employment, 38 per cent were with professors, and 12 per cent were with other officials of the college. Seventy-one per cent of the conferences were reported helpful; 29 per cent were not. The state of solutions of the problem is reported as follows:

	Number	Per Cent
Satisfactorily solved	67	44
Partially solved	12	8
Unsolved	51	34
No solution indicated	22	14

PROBLEMS OF PART-TIME WORK AS INDICATED IN THE STUDENT
INTERVIEWS

One hundred thirty students who were interviewed do not have problems of part-time work for the following reasons:

60 have sufficient funds without working
33 have full-time positions
26 prefer to borrow
11 are not allowed to do part-time work on account of holding fellowships or scholarships

Ten of the 11 students who state they have had problems of part-time work in past years have solved their problems satisfactorily.

Of the 85 students in the interview group who have had problems of part-time work this year, 42 have obtained positions which meet their needs, and 43 have not. Of the group who have solved their problems of part-time work, 11 can continue through the year without the work, 31 cannot. Of the group who have not obtained work, 18 can continue through the year without it, 19 cannot continue, and 6 are uncertain whether they can or not.

Twenty-eight (65 per cent) of the group of 43 students who have not been able to solve their problems of part-time work satisfactorily give as the reason for their failure "inability to obtain any work." Other reasons given and their frequencies are:

5 have obtained insufficient amounts of work
3 have conflicts between part-time work and academic work
3 receive insufficient pay for the amount of work done
2 have work of an undesirable kind
2 need work but have no time for it

Of the 83 students who have had problems of part-time work this year, 23 state that they have consulted the Bureau of Part-Time Employment with regard to the problem. Four of the 23 have secured satisfactory work through the Bureau, 5 have secured an occasional job, and 14 have secured no work.

Type of Position Held. The amount of remunerative work carried by students in addition to their academic load ranges from an hour or two a day to a full-time position. Students holding full-time teaching positions are not included in this discussion of part-time work. Sixty-four of the 215 students interviewed are holding part-time positions. The type of part-time work most frequently done is teaching, 18 being engaged in this type of work. If assisting and tutoring are included in this classification, the number is increased to 30, nearly one-half of all the part-time positions. The positions held, in the order of their frequency, are as follows:

	Number		Number
Teaching	18	Clerical work	1
Assisting	9	Desk duty	1
Dining-hall duty	5	Health service	1
Caring for children	5	Lecturing	1
Religious work	4	Serving	1
Post office	4	Singing in choir	1
Tutoring	3	Typing	1
Domestic service	3	Odd jobs	1
Clerking	2	Office work	1
Club work	2		

This group of 64 students report as follows regarding the length of time that they work a week:

1 is working under 5 hours a week
10 are working from 5–9 hours a week
19 are working from 10–14 hours a week
5 are working from 15–19 hours a week
9 are working from 20–24 hours a week
2 are working from 25–29 hours a week
4 are working from 30–39 hours a week
3 are working 40 or more hours a week
11 are working irregularly

Two of the 7 students who are working 30 hours a week or more are assistants to professors, 2 are working in the post office, one is working in a dining hall, one is doing office work, and one is doing religious work.

Remuneration Received. Twenty-one students are engaged on a yearly basis. The highest salary earned by anyone in this group is by a man, a graduate student in psychology, who receives $200 a month for caring for a child. Six other students are earning $1,500 a year or more. Two of these 6 are assisting professors, 2 are doing religious work, 1 is teaching, and 1 is working in the post office. Six are earning from $1,000 to $1,499 a year, 4 from $500 to $999, and 4 earn under $500.

Twenty-seven students are paid on a weekly basis. Four of this group earn $30 a week or over. Two of these 4 are working in the post office and 2 are teaching. The salary most frequently received by this group of 27 students is less than $5 a week.

Seven students work for some portion or all of their living expenses. The remaining 9 work intermittently with no stated salary. With the exception of those students who have salaried positions in the fields of teaching, assisting, religious work, and post office work, the remuneration received from the part-time positions seems insufficient to repay for the expenditure of time required. One boy, for example, a graduate student, is working as clerk 20 hours a week in a large grocery store for $6. One girl, also a graduate student, is working 15 hours a week in a well-known restaurant for $4.50.

Value of Positions to Professional Advancement of Students. Thirty-six students consider that their part-time work contributes to their professional advancement, 5 consider that it does to some extent, and 23 think it does not contribute at all. In general, those positions which are paid best are also the ones which contribute to the student's professional advancement. However, 2 of the assistants and 2 students who are teaching state that their present work is of no value to them professionally.

Agencies Through Which Positions Are Obtained. Table X shows the agencies through which students report that they have secured part-time positions. It should be remembered that full-time teaching positions are not included in this group, which is the reason for not mentioning the Bureau of Educational Service as an agency.

Twenty of the 64 positions were secured through professors, 20 through the efforts of the individuals themselves, 14 through the Bureau of Part-Time Employment, 7 through friends, 2 through agencies outside the college, and 1 through an officer of the college. Here again the important part played by the faculty in extra-classroom services to students is apparent. Eight of the 9 assisting positions and 8 of the 18 teaching positions were secured through professors. Nineteen of the 21 students who are employed by the year secured their positions through the assistance of professors.

TABLE X

AGENCIES THROUGH WHICH STUDENTS REPORT THAT THEY HAVE
SECURED PART-TIME WORK

POSITION	NUMBER OF STUDENTS REPORTING THAT THEY HAVE SECURED POSITIONS THROUGH						
	Pro-fessors	Other Officers of the College	Bureau of Part-Time Employ-ment	Self	Friends	Others outside College	Total
Assisting	8	0	0	0	1	0	9
Caring for chil-dren	1	0	2	2	0	0	5
Clerking	0	0	0	2	0	0	2
Clerical	0	0	1	0	0	0	1
Club work	1	0	0	0	1	0	2
Desk duty	0	0	0	1	0	0	1
Dining halls	0	0	3	1	1	0	5
Domestic service	0	0	2	1	0	0	3
Health service ..	0	0	0	1	0	0	1
Lecturing	0	0	0	0	0	1	1
Odd jobs	0	0	0	1	0	0	1
Office work	0	1	0	0	0	0	1
Post office	0	0	0	3	1	0	4
Religious work ..	2	0	0	0	1	1	4
Serving	0	0	1	0	0	0	1
Singing in choir .	0	0	0	1	0	0	1
Teaching	8	0	2	6	2	0	18
Tutoring	0	0	2	1	0	0	3
Typing	0	0	1	0	0	0	1
Total	20	1	14	20	7	2	64

The positions secured through the Bureau of Part-Time Employment appear to be on the whole routine in type and not of a highly skilled nature.

SUMMARY

Of the problems relating to part-time work, the difficulty of actually obtaining the work is mentioned most frequently. Forty-four per cent of students reporting problems of part-time work on the Student Inquiry Blanks have found positions which meet their needs. Thirty-four per cent have found no solution to their problems of part-time work.

In the group of 215 students interviewed, 64 are holding part-time positions. The positions most frequently held are part-time teaching and assisting. Forty-one of the 64 students who are working part time consider that their work contributes in some degree to their professional advancement. Twenty-three consider their work of no advantage professionally. In general, those positions which contribute to the student's professional development are also the best paid. A number of students are doing work which is routine in type, and poorly paid.

Part-time positions are secured both through professors and through the Bureau of Part-Time Employment. Sixteen of the 27 teaching and assisting positions were secured through professors. Work secured through the Bureau of Part-Time Employment is in general less highly skilled and less remunerative than work secured through professors.

Chapter VIII

PROBLEMS OF PLACEMENT

THE question of vocational placement is an important one with professional students. Judging by the prevalence of financial problems in the group studied, many students find considerable difficulty in financing their professional study and must obtain work as soon as possible after completing their period of study. Since their vocation is one of the paramount interests of professional students and since much of their happiness is bound up with being able to do work which is satisfying to them, the importance to them of securing positions which offer adequate opportunity for developing their abilities and interests can hardly be overemphasized. It is of importance to the college also, since much of its reputation rests upon the professional success of its graduates. The present chapter deals with problems of placement from the standpoint of the students.

PROBLEMS OF PLACEMENT AS SHOWN IN THE STUDENT INQUIRY
BLANKS

Prevalence and Kinds of Problems. One hundred fifty students report placement as a major problem. One hundred thirty-two mention problems of future vocational placement; 9, problems of obtaining placement at once; and 9, past problems of placement. Only 12 of the 132 problems of future placement involve problems other than the problem of obtaining a position. They are:

	Number
Shall I return to my present position or seek a new one?	3
Difficulty in securing placement on account of race	3
What type of position shall I apply for?	1
Shall I accept a position I am not well prepared for?	1
Shall I accept an assistantship in the college or a permanent position elsewhere?	1
I desire placement in Panama	1
I have a position now; shall I register with the Bureau of Educational Service?	1
Shall I accept position offered me which I do not care for?	1

Problems Mentioned by Different Groups. Problems of placement are mentioned by all groups. They are, however, more
frequent among full-time than among part-time students. Over
one-fourth of all full-time men students report the problem. Students under 25 years of age and over 45 cite it more often than
those in the other age groups. It is reported as a major problem
by 17.4 per cent of graduate students, but by only 8.8 per cent
of undergraduates. Men list it more frequently than women;
19.5 per cent of men and 13.5 per cent of women report it.

Consultations Concerning Placement. The agency maintained
by the college to assist students in securing positions is known
as the Bureau of Educational Service. Any student who is taking
or has completed 12 points of work or more is entitled to register
with this Bureau. Forty-six per cent of students reporting the
problem of placement have already consulted with a college officer
regarding it. Sixty-six students report 101 conferences. Fifty-
six of these conferences have been with professors, 32 have been
with the staff of the Bureau, and 13 have been with other officials
in the college. If the students had reported later in the academic
year, the number of conferences with the Bureau would, of course,
have been much higher. In November many students have hardly
begun to consider seriously the problem of placement for the following year. It is of interest to note the large number of conferences reported with professors. Fifty-five per cent of all conferences reported on placement problems are with members of the
faculty.

PROBLEMS OF PLACEMENT AS SHOWN BY STUDENT INTERVIEWS

Prevalence and Kinds of Problems. The student interviews
were planned to answer the following questions regarding placement problems:

1. Is the problem one of obtaining some kind of position or of
obtaining a better position than the one held at present?

2. Does the student want placement in the same kind of work
he has been doing or does he desire a change?

3. What were his reasons for leaving his last position?

4. When does he desire placement?

5. How much educational experience has he had?

6. What steps has he taken toward securing a position?

In the interview group, in the case of problems such as finance, the decision as to whether or not the student had a financial problem rested with him. In the matter of placement, however, any student who had no position at the time of the interview and no promise of any and needed a position by September, 1932, was considered to have a problem of placement.

Eighty-nine students (41 per cent) of the 215 interviewed have no placement problem for the following reasons:

25 are on leave of absence and expect to return to their present positions
40 are holding satisfactory positions now
17 expect to remain in school another year
 7 are foreign students who plan to return to their native lands

Of the one hundred twenty-six students (59 per cent) who have placement problems, 114 have the problem of obtaining a position. Only 12 have the problem of obtaining a better position than the one they now have. Fifty-seven per cent of those who have had experience want placement in the same kind of work they have been doing; 43 per cent wish a different type of work. Practically all are majoring in the field in which they hope to work.

A recent investigation by Hager[1] gives information bearing on the possibilities of obtaining employment in a new field of educational work. His results indicate that persons who attempt a change in type of work following a year of graduate study are generally unsuccessful in obtaining a position in the field of graduate specialization. During the first year after receiving the Master's degree, 34 per cent of the group studied obtained a position for which the major work may have been a preparation. During the fifth year after that award, 37 per cent were so engaged. Practically one-half of those who attempted changes returned to the type of position held immediately before receiving the Master's degree. Individuals who specialized in subject matter fields were most successful in effecting changes.

Summing up his findings, Hager states: "After a person has had five years experience in one field, it is often very difficult for him to make a change deliberately following a year of graduate training for the desired type of work."[2] In view of this study, it seems probable that a number of the 44 students who desire to change the type of work they have been doing will not be able to make the change.

[1] Walter E. Hager, *The Quest for Vocational Adjustment in the Profession of Education.* Contributions to Education, No. 491. New York: Bureau of Publications, Teachers College, Columbia University, 1932. [2] *Ibid.*

Information such as that obtained by Hager[3] should be of considerable benefit to students at the time when they are beginning their graduate work and are considering their choice of courses and major.

Eight students (6 per cent) need placement at once, 23 (18 per cent) wish it at the end of the current semester, 11 (9 per cent), in June, and 84 (67 per cent), in September.

Characteristics of the Group Citing Problems of Placement. Fifty-three per cent of all students interviewed are without a position and need placement not later than September, 1932. The group of 114 students having this problem shows the following characteristics:

> 5 are full-time women students working for Ph.D. degree
> 10 are full-time men students working for Ph.D. degree
> 34 are full-time women students working for M.A. degree
> 20 are full-time men students working for M.A. degree
> 12 are full-time women students working for B.S. degree
>
> 6 are part-time women students working for Ph.D. degree
> 11 are part-time men students working for Ph.D. degree
> 10 are part-time women students working for M.A. degree
> 4 are part-time men students working for M.A. degree
> 2 are part-time women students working for B.S. degree

Seventy-one per cent of the group desiring positions are full-time students; 47 per cent are full-time students working for the Master's degree. Sixty per cent of all students needing placement are working for the Master's degree. This is 6 per cent higher than the percentage of students in the entire group working for the Master's degree. In other words, the problem of placement in the group interviewed is slightly more acute with candidates for the Master's degree than with students working for other degrees.

Among students desiring placement it is of interest to note the concentration of men in the groups working for graduate degrees. No men are in the group working for the Bachelor's degree; 24 of the 68 working for the Master's degree and 21 of the 32 working toward the Doctor's degree are men.

As Table XI shows, one-fifth of the group having placement problems have had no teaching experience; one-half have had from one to 9 years; one-fourth, from 10 to 19 years; and 5 per cent, 20 years or more. The largest number of people have apparently

[3] *Ibid.*

TABLE XI

EDUCATIONAL EXPERIENCE OF 126 STUDENTS HAVING
PROBLEMS OF PLACEMENT

NUMBER OF YEARS' TEACHING EXPERIENCE	NUMBER	PER CENT
0	25	20
1–4	27	22
5–9	37	29
10–14	22	17
15–19	9	7
20 and over	6	5

either become dissatisfied with their positions, or demonstrated their inability to fill them, in 5 to 9 years.

Present Status in Regard to a Position. Information was obtained from 115 students concerning their present status with regard to a position. Seventy-two had resigned from their previous positions; 18 had lost their previous positions. Of the latter group, 13 lost their positions because of reductions in expenditures in the school system; 5 were on temporary appointments. Twenty-five have never held positions.

Reasons for Leaving Previous Position. In spite of the fact that the college does not assure students of placement following their period of study, 72 of the 126 have resigned from their positions before beginning study. Reasons for resignations were given as follows:

31 hoped for better positions
24 resigned to continue study
6 resigned due to illness
5 resigned because work or associates were uncongenial
3 resigned because of a salary cut
3 resigned under pressure

Three-fourths have apparently left their previous positions mainly because they believe their graduate study will enable them to obtain better positions. Nearly one-half of these students are in the age group from 35 to 44. The Bureau of Educational Service in its printed material definitely advises educational workers nearing the forties not to resign positions until they are reasonably sure of obtaining new ones. It recommends that persons 35 and over do their graduate work in summer sessions or while on leave of absence.

Consultations Concerning Placement. Thirty-six of the 114 students from whom information was obtained have completed registration with the Bureau of Educational Service, 20 have consulted the Bureau but have not yet filed their papers, and 58 have not consulted the Bureau. Thirty-three of the 58 who have not consulted the Bureau are new students who have been in school just two months. Since the Bureau requires letters of recommendation from local professors, many new students wait until they have completed at least one semester in the college before registering with the Bureau and asking professors for recommendations. This fact accounts in part for the relatively small percentage of students needing a position who have registered with the Bureau.

Outside of consulting the Bureau, few students have as yet made efforts to solve their placement problems. Twenty-nine are registered with outside agencies; most of these students maintain a permanent registration with these agencies. Eleven have applied for positions by letter, 6 have made personal application, and 3 have had the aid of friends. The others report that they have done nothing toward solving their placement problems. Only 10 per cent have any definite position in mind which they hope to obtain after the completion of their work.

SUMMARY

Fifteen per cent of the students returning the Student Inquiry Blanks cite placement as a major problem. Over one-half of the group interviewed, however, are not on leave of absence, have no position in mind after finishing their study, and need a position not later than September, 1932. A possible reason for the apparent discrepancy between questionnaire and interview results is that in filling out the Student Inquiry Blanks early in the Fall students did not think of their need of a position at the end of their period of study, even though all the conditions revealed in the interview existed.

Students rely for placement mainly on the Bureau of Educational Service maintained by the college. However, at the time of the interviews (November 1931), 46 per cent had not yet consulted the Bureau. The majority expect to secure placement after their second semester of graduate study.

Fifty-seven per cent of the students interviewed who have placement problems have resigned from their previous positions.

In view of the oversupply of teachers in the country, students appear to overemphasize the efficacy of graduate training in securing a position. Forty-three per cent of students having previous educational experience wish to change their type of work. That many will not be able to secure a position in the new field seems probable in view of recent research which shows the difficulty of making such a change following a year of graduate training.

Chapter IX

PROBLEMS OF SOCIAL RELATIONSHIPS

In a student body as heterogeneous as the one under consideration many problems in social relationships may be expected. Certain factors, in particular, create problems. The mingling of many races and nationalities brings about problems which would not arise in a more homogeneous group. The wide variation in age calls for adjustments on the part of both the younger and the older students. The fact that the women outnumber the men three to one in itself creates an abnormal social situation. When one considers also that 45 per cent of the men are married, in comparison with 15 per cent of the women, the complexity of the problem becomes still more apparent.

PROBLEMS OF SOCIAL RELATIONSHIPS AS SHOWN IN THE STUDENT INQUIRY BLANKS

Prevalence of Problems in Different Groups. One hundred thirty-two students of the group of 1,000 report problems in social relationships. Women mention problems in this field more frequently than men. Part-time women students give them first place. The most outstanding difference is found between the married and the single groups; 4.5 per cent of the married group and 15.7 per cent of the single group cite problems of this nature. Students under 25 years of age mention difficulties in this area more frequently than students in any of the other age groups; students from 35 to 44 years of age, least frequently.

Frequency of Specific Problems. The many kinds of specific problems reported may be seen from the following list:

	Number
Lack of normal social life	21
Desire for contacts with people of similar interests	17
Few contacts with opposite sex	11
Few opportunities to associate with younger people	5
Few opportunities of meeting people	4

Whether to marry	4
Lack of time for social relationships	3
Lack of acquaintances	2
Social relationships hampered by race prejudice	2
Relationships with foreign students	2
Social relationships hampered by lack of money	2
Desire to join an Italian club	1
Difficulty in adjusting to associating with older people	1
How can one learn to be tolerant?	1
Desire for contact with Americans	1
How may I gain the cooperation of fellow workers?	1
How much time shall I devote to social life?	1
Need to overcome inclination to be too much alone	1
Want to find a roommate	1
Desire contacts outside the college	1
Social relationships (specific problem not stated)	50
Total	132

Consultation on Problems. Very few students report conferences with any college official on problems of social relationships. Only 14 conferences are reported. They are with the following officials:

	Number
Professors	5
Welfare Director and staff	5
Secretary of Student Organizations	3
Friend in the college	1

Personnel officers such as the Welfare Director and her staff and the Executive Secretary of Student Organizations have, as shown by their interview records, a number of conferences with students on various phases of social relationships. However, according to students' reports they consult these officers few times on problems which they regard as major ones in this field.

Solutions Reported. Forty per cent of students reporting problems of social relationships indicate that these problems are still unsolved. Ways in which students are attempting to solve this type of problem are:

> Live in a college dormitory
> Live in International House
> Attend Graduate Club
> Attend departmental club
> Join outside organizations
> Seek friends outside the college
> Make efforts to meet people
> Ignore the problem

PROBLEMS OF SOCIAL RELATIONSHIPS AS SHOWN BY STUDENT
INTERVIEWS

Purpose of the Interviews. The interviews were designed to
secure a better analysis of the problems of social relationships, of
the factors giving rise to the problems, and of the efforts being
made to solve them, and to obtain students' suggestions for improving the present situation.

Prevalence of Different Problems. One hundred ten students
of the 215 in the interview group consider that they have problems
in this field; 105 consider that their problems are either being
satisfactorily met or that they have no problems. Specific problems reported are:

	Number
Difficulty in making social contacts	35
Lack of contacts with fellow students	26
Lack of contacts with the opposite sex	23
Lack of contacts with interesting people	7
Lack of contacts with students outside own field	6
Lack of contacts with people one's own age	6
Too many social contacts	2
Delayed marriage	2
Lack of social contacts with professors	1
Difficulty in managing social contacts	1
Lack of contacts with friends	1

Twenty-two of the 23 students citing the problem of lack of social
contacts with the opposite sex are women; 18 are full-time women
students. Only two of the entire group consider that they have
problems arising from too many social contacts.

Factors Underlying Problems. Causes of problems of social relationships are of three types. Two of these pertain to the individual himself and the third relates to his social environment. Of
the two relating primarily to the individual, one is due to factors
external to himself, such as lack of time for making social contacts, lack of money, or lack of facilities for entertaining, referred
to as Type A. The other, which may be termed lack of ability to
make social contacts, is due to factors inherent in his training,
experience, or heredity, Type B. The third, over which the college has a measure of control, is that of opportunities offered for
social contacts, Type C. When grouped under the above heading,
the 126 reasons given for difficulties in this area are:

	Number	Per Cent
Type A—Problems due to factors external to the individual	64	50.8
Type B—Problems due to factors inherent in the individual	17	13.5
Type C—Problems due to social environment	45	35.7

Reasons given for difficulties of Type A, which account for 51 per cent of all problems listed, are:

	Number
Lack of time	55
Lack of money	5
Commuting	2
Lack of facilities for entertaining	2

Causes of difficulty of Type B, in which the problems are due to factors inherent in the individual, are:

	Number
Lack of ability to make social contacts	12
Race a handicap to social contacts	2
Lack of energy	2
Physical handicap	1

The 45 difficulties of Type C are all due to lack of opportunities for social contacts. Thirty-six of those stating lack of opportunities as the cause of their problems are full-time students.

Summing up the causes of difficulty, one finds that 64 per cent of problems of this kind are due to factors directly pertaining to the individual and 36 per cent, to factors which may involve the social direction of the college.

Social Participation of Interview Group. The organization to which all students of the college are eligible for membership is known as the Graduate Club. Two-thirds of the students state that up to the present time they have attended no meetings of this club; one-third have attended some meetings.

More popular than a club whose membership is composed of a cross section of the student group are the professional clubs in specific major fields. Fifty-nine per cent of students attend the professional clubs. Eighty-eight per cent attend one-half or more of the meetings.

That students do not limit their social participation wholly to college organizations is shown by the fact that over one-fourth of them belong to social organizations outside the college.

Suggestions for Improvement of Social Situation. The request most frequently made by students is for small informal gatherings of people of like interests. They express the feeling that when they take time to attend a social function, they wish something more than a cup of tea. They want informal discussion with people having interests similar to their own. They would like the opportunity of meeting professors as well as students in this way. Statements such as the following are typical of the suggestions made:

I should like some way of getting acquainted with people interested in the same kind of work I am interested in.

I should like small discussion groups for people of the same interests.

Meetings of small groups of students and professors interested in special fields would be of great benefit to students.

I should like more contacts such as the German universities offer. I feel the need of informal contacts with people as human beings rather than with their pedagogical labels.

I should appreciate the opportunity to get acquainted with some of the professors early in the year. If I could have met my professors socially, it would have changed my whole attitude toward my work.

Other requests frequently made are for social gatherings early in the year and for a room where men and women may gather for informal sociability. Requests made less frequently are for a student club to discuss spiritual questions, social leadership for the alumni of the college, and more social affairs such as dances.

SUMMARY AND DISCUSSION

Problems of social relationships are especially important because much of the individual's happiness depends upon his ability to achieve a satisfactory adjustment in this area. The fact that 40 per cent of the students reporting social problems have found no solution for them suggests the need of a more adequate social program than exists in the institution at present.

Practically all the problems in this field arise from lack of social contacts. Only two of the 132 problems of social relationships cited in the Student Inquiry Blanks involve too many social contacts.

Students consider factors, such as lack of time and, less frequently, lack of money, responsible for half of their problems of social relationships; factors inherent in themselves, such as lack of ability to make social contacts, responsible for 13 per cent of their difficulties; and the social environment in which they are placed, the cause of slightly over one-third of their problems.

Many of the problems cited in the field of social relationships are inherent in the nature of the student body. For example, one problem often mentioned by full-time women students is lack of social contacts with men. It is difficult to see how the college can assist very much in solving this type of problem as long as the women outnumber the men three to one.

A larger number of informal social affairs for small groups of students and faculty members sponsored by the college would meet a need felt by many students. Contacts of this kind would assist in the solution of problems caused by lack of opportunity for meeting fellow students and professors in a social way.

Changing the social environment alone will not solve problems of social relationships. Opportunities may be provided, but unless the student can find time to attend social affairs and is interested in attending them, the social program will fail.

Chapter X

PROBLEMS OF LEISURE AND RECREATION

THE growing interest in the wise use of leisure time is indicated by the increasing number of articles and books on the subject which have been appearing recently. The *Journal of the National Education Association*, in particular, has devoted a large amount of space to various phases of the question.

A wise use of leisure time is essential to the teacher's happiness and to his professional success. It is of benefit to the individual himself in sustaining his zest for life by giving him interests through which physical and mental energy may be restored. Viscount Grey[1] includes among his four essentials for happiness "some degree of leisure and the use of it in some way that makes us happy."

The maintenance of a wholesome, happy outlook on life on the part of the individual preparing to teach is of vital importance. Students quickly react to the mental attitude of the teacher. A teacher habitually tired and discouraged cannot create in his classroom the kind of atmosphere essential to constructive work.

Teachers who have developed for themselves a satisfying program of leisure activities can establish a sense of the values of life in the mind of each pupil and assist him in cultivating creative leisure interests better than teachers who have forgotten how to play.

PROBLEMS OF LEISURE AND RECREATION AS SHOWN IN THE
STUDENT INQUIRY BLANKS

Prevalence and Kinds of Problems. That students are cognizant of problems in the field of leisure and recreation is indicated by the fact that 155 of the 1,000 students who returned the Student Inquiry Blanks report problems of this type. They are second in frequency of all personal problems reported. Full-time women students and the full-time anonymous group mention problems of leisure more frequently than any other problem.

[1] Viscount Grey of Fallodon, *Recreation*, p. 4. Boston: Houghton Mifflin Company, 1920.

The specific problems reported, with the number of students reporting each problem, are:

	Number
Lack of time for recreation	76
How to use leisure time profitably	26
No place for recreation	16
Lack of physical exercise	15
How arrange work to allow for leisure	6
Information concerning leisure opportunities in the city	4
Amount of time to allow for recreation	3
Desirable forms of recreation in the city	3
Lack of recreational facilities at convenient hours	3
Where find inexpensive recreation?	2
Recreation for children	1

It will be seen that the problem reported by nearly one-half of the 155 students is lack of time for leisure and recreation.

Consultation on Problems. Only 19 students (12 per cent) report that they have consulted anyone about problems of this nature. Twenty-one consultations are reported with the following officials:

	Number
Professors	11
Members of physical education department	3
Social directors of dormitories	3
Doctor	1
Others	3

Eighty-six per cent of the conferences are considered helpful.

Degree to Which Problems Have Been Solved. The problems in the field of leisure and recreation are reported solved to the following degrees:

	Number	Per Cent
Partially solved	11	7.1
Attempting a solution	46	29.7
Unsolved	62	40.0
No solution indicated	36	23.2

PROBLEMS OF LEISURE AND RECREATION AS REVEALED IN STUDENT INTERVIEWS

The student interviews offered an opportunity to study the problems of leisure and recreation more carefully. Their purpose was to ascertain the specific problems in this field and the causes of the problems as stated by the students, the facilities offered by the college which they are using, additional facilities which they would like, the forms of recreation in which they engage, and whether or not they follow definite time schedules. (See Appendix B.)

Prevalence and Kinds of Problems. Of 215 students interviewed 82 report that they have no problems of this nature. The 133 who do have problems in this area report the following specific difficulties:

	Number
Lack of time for recreation	96
Lack of facilities for recreation	13
Lack of companion for recreation	7
How to use leisure time	6
Lack of money for recreation	6
Lack of energy for recreation	5

Causes of Problems. The percentage of students in the interview groups who consider their problem that of lack of time for recreation is 72. This percentage is even higher than that in the Student Inquiry Blanks. The reasons given by students for their lack of time for recreation are:

	Number
Pressure of academic work	61
Working part-time	23
Working full-time	13
Poor budgeting of time	8
Commuting	5
Housekeeping duties	4

In the opinion of 54 per cent of these students, pressure of academic work accounts for their lack of time for recreation. Pressure of academic work is given as the cause of lack of leisure time by 36 per cent of full-time students and 14 per cent of part-time students. Forty-one per cent of full-time women students regard it as the cause of their leisure problems. Part-time and full-time work together account for the problems of 31 per cent of the group. Only 8 (7 per cent) of the students attribute their difficulties to poor budgeting of time.

Facilities of the College Used by Students. Information on this point was obtained from 167 students in interviews. Of these

130 (78 per cent) are using none of the following facilities offered by the college for recreation: swimming pool, gymnasium, volley ball and handball courts.

The facility most frequently used is the gymnasium, including volley ball and handball courts. The swimming pool is used by the second largest number. Nine students state that they would like to use the swimming pool and gymnasium, but find the hours inconvenient.

Facilities for Recreation Which Students Would Like. Most of the students state that they have no time to use the recreational facilities now available and therefore are not interested in having others. The following facilities were requested by the number of students indicated:

	Number
Tennis courts	19
Swimming pool open longer hours	6
Bowling	5
Indoor sports	5
Recreational gymnasium class	5
Gymnasium open for use more often	4
Volley ball	2
More equipment in the gymnasium	1

Forms of Recreation Engaged In. The interview group consisted of 143 women and 72 men. They report that they engage in the following kinds of recreation:

	Men	Women	Total
Walking	19	55	74
Theaters and concerts	13	25	38
Reading	4	4	8
Swimming	1	5	6
Tennis	3	3	6
Gymnasium	3	3	6
Trips	0	6	6
Dancing	0	6	6
Museum and art exhibits	0	4	4
Cards	0	2	2
Others—dinners, music, golf, radio, etc.	10	13	23

Number of Students Who Follow Time Budgets. Two-thirds of the students report that they follow definite time budgets. Most of them are worked out by the week. The percentage of students who report that they work on definite time budgets is the same for the group to whom leisure and recreation is a problem as for the group who do not consider it a problem.

PROBLEMS OF LEISURE AND RECREATION AS REVEALED IN THE
STUDENT TIME SCHEDULES

Both the Student Inquiry Blanks and the interviews with students indicate the prevalence of problems of leisure. The specific problem mentioned most frequently is lack of time for leisure. Over one-half of the students who state in the interviews that their problem is lack of leisure attribute their lack of leisure to the pressure of academic work.

Some means of verifying these expressions of students regarding their problems in this area seemed desirable. Financial problems could be verified in the interviews. For example, if a student stated that he had a financial problem, his judgment could be checked by ascertaining whether he was borrowing money, working part-time, or reducing his expenses to a minimum. With the question of leisure time, however, it was impossible to do more than gain a further expression of opinion through the interview.

The student time schedules were used to obtain objective information with regard to the following questions:

1. How much leisure time do students have?
2. Do students who state that they have problems in this area have less leisure time than other students?
3. How much time are students spending on academic work?
4. What other activities are encroaching on leisure time?
5. In what recreational activities are students engaging?

Since the main purpose of the time schedules was to obtain more detailed and more accurate information regarding leisure activities, students were asked to state specifically in the schedules the forms of recreation and leisure activities in which they engaged. The following activities reported by students were classed under the heading of leisure-time activities:

Rest	Newspaper reading
Walking	Attendance at theaters
Participation in sports and	Attendance at concerts
games	Attendance at the opera
Recreational reading	Attendance at movies

Attendance at lectures	Trips, motoring
Attendance at museums and	Letter writing
exhibits	Informal sociability—visiting
Auditing classes	Formal social affairs—dinners,
Listening to radio	parties
Spectator at games and sports	Miscellaneous recreation

1. *How Much Leisure Time Have Students?* The proportion of students' time which on the average is devoted to leisure-time activities may be seen in Chart I. The average number of minutes devoted to various activities is indicated in Tables XIIA, XIIB, and XIIC. Full-time and part-time students have on the

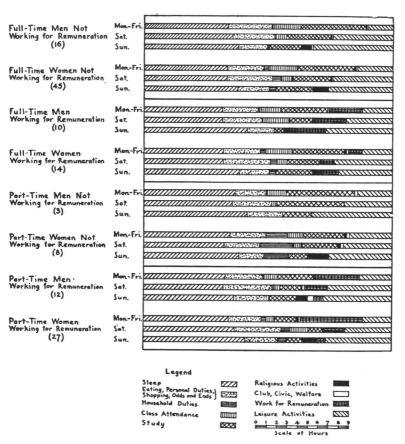

CHART I. Activities of 135 Students During a 24-Hour Day, Based on Records Kept for One Week

PROBLEMS OF STUDENTS

TABLE XIIA

AVERAGE NUMBER OF MINUTES PER DAY DEVOTED TO VARIOUS
ACTIVITIES BY 135 STUDENTS DURING A FIVE-DAY WEEK

GROUP	NO.	ACTIVITY								
		Sleep	Eating, Personal Duties	House-hold Duties	Class	Study	Religious Activities	Club, Civic, Welfare	Remunerative Work	Leisure
Full-time										
Total	85	476	210	39	165	327	10	6	123	191
Not working										
Men	16	488	217	8	159	382	9	1		176
Women ...	45	480	210	28	175	329	10	5		203
Working										
Men	10	456	202	1	140	266		8	189	178
Women ...	14	465	206	28	159	302	9	13	77	181
Part-time										
Total	50	486	197	38	65	180	12	8	337	193
Not working										
Men	3	529	176	9	105	403		11		207
Women ...	8	501	200	132	89	239	10	7		252
Working										
Men	12	469	216	6	80	206	3	5	268	187
Women ...	27	485	190	28	46	126	13	9	365	178
Total	135	480	205	27	128	273	11	7	255	192

average the same amount of leisure time from Monday through Friday—3.2 hours per day. On Saturday there is a decided increase in the amount of leisure time of both groups, full-time students having 5.7 hours of leisure and part-time students, 5.1 hours. The largest amount of leisure time for both groups comes on Sunday. Full-time students have 6.4 hours of leisure on Sunday and part-time students, 6.6. The amount of time spent on the average in leisure activities during the seven-day week by the entire group of students is 4 hours.

Full-time women students spend 3.1 hours a day in leisure during the five-day week. This is the group reporting problems of leisure most frequently in the Student Inquiry Blanks. In comparison with other groups, full-time women students have on the average more time per day for leisure activities than any other group except part-time women students not working for remuneration.

It is interesting to speculate as to the reason why full-time

TABLE XIIB
AVERAGE NUMBER OF MINUTES DEVOTED TO VARIOUS ACTIVITIES
ON SATURDAY BY 135 STUDENTS

GROUP	NO.	ACTIVITY								
		Sleep	Eating, Personal Duties	House-hold Duties	Class	Study	Religious Activities	Club, Civic, Welfare	Remunerative Work	Leisure
Full-time										
Total	85	482	253	41	69	217	5	2	126	342
Not working										
Men	16	513	239	11	39	279	6	5		348
Women ...	45	482	260	47	70	223	3	1		354
Working										
Men	10	457	247		134	130			200	272
Women ...	14	466	254	54	52	188	8		74	344
Part-time										
Total	50	485	269	65	73	152	5	12	125	305
Not working										
Men	3	517	210		40	380			80	272
Women ...	8	465	201	194	52	208	15	11		294
Working										
Men	12	457	282	12	34	123	1	10	123	380
Women ...	27	500	290	50	100	87	3	5	126	279
Total	135	483	258	50	70	186	5	6	126	327

women students report problems of this nature in the question-naires more frequently than other groups. It may be that 3 hours a day from Monday to Friday actually is too little leisure time and that this group is more cognizant of the problem than other groups. On the other hand, it may not be the absolute amount of time which is creating the problem, but the divisions into which leisure time falls. Since 97 per cent of this group attend class or study on Saturday and 78 per cent study on Sunday, there is no day in the week which is free from academic work for any large percentage of the group. A third possible explanation is that full-time women students expect to have considerable leisure time during their residence at the college. Many have been teaching for a number of years and may hope to have time during their year in school to enjoy many of the cultural opportunities afforded by a large city.

Full-time women students not working for remuneration spend 3.4 hours a day in leisure during the five-day week and full-time

TABLE XIIC
AVERAGE NUMBER OF MINUTES DEVOTED TO VARIOUS ACTIVITIES ON SUNDAY BY 135 STUDENTS

GROUP	NO.	ACTIVITY								
		Sleep	Eating, Personal Duties	Household Duties	Class	Study	Religious Activities	Club, Civic, Welfare	Remunerative Work	Leisure
Full-time										
Total	85	546	172	34		190	74	11	150	382
Not working										
Men	16	544	165	4		192	62	11		462
Women ...	45	544	172	42		213	96			373
Working										
Men	10	559	195			56	18		221	391
Women ...	14	551	164	41		210	58		101	315
Part-time										
Total	50	599	187	61		99	89	15	61	394
Not working										
Men	3	589	199			171				481
Women ...	8	543	147	145		113	119			373
Working										
Men	12	520	202	2		132	65	34	85	400
Women ...	27	578	191	62		73	91	7	50	388
Total	135	551	177	44		156	79	23	95	387

women students who are working for remuneration spend 3 hours a day. The full-time women group who are not working for remuneration have hardly any more leisure time on Saturday than those who are working. They do, however, have almost an hour more leisure time on Sunday. Part-time women students not working for remuneration have on the average the largest amount of leisure time during the five-day week.

Full-time men students who are working for remuneration spend on the average the same amount of time in leisure-time activities as full-time men students not working for remuneration, namely, 2.9 hours. The full-time men group who are not working have approximately 1.2 hours more leisure time on both Saturday and Sunday than those who are working.

It is difficult to know whether or not these are reasonable amounts of leisure time for the groups of students concerned. There are no well-defined standards of the amount of leisure time which is desirable for students. Suzzallo,[2] writing on the sub-

[2] Henry Suzzallo, "The Use of Leisure," *Journal of the National Education Association*, XIX (April 1930), 124.

ject of leisure for adults, suggests that five hours a day is a fair amount of time to devote to leisure. The 135 students who kept the schedules spend on the average one hour a day less in leisure than this suggested amount.

2. *Do Students Who State That They Have Problems of Leisure and Recreation Have Less Leisure Time Than Other Students?* In the group keeping the schedules, both men and women who stated that they had problems of leisure spent less time in leisure-time activities than the students who did not state problems.

The 60 women who stated in the interviews that they had problems of leisure and recreation spent on the average 26.6 hours in recreation during the 7 days in which the schedules were kept. The 32 women who did not state problems in this area spent on the average 30 hours in recreation. The former group spent on the average 3.8 hours a day; the latter group spent on the average 4.3 hours a day. Apparently the group of students who report leisure-time problems actually have less time for recreation than those who report no problems of this type.

The men who listed problems of recreation spent an average of 25.4 hours a week in recreation, in comparison with 33.9 hours for the men who did not state such problems.

3. *How Much Time Are Students Spending on Academic Work?* The amount of time spent on academic work by various groups among the 135 students who kept time schedules is given in detail in Table XIII. The amount of time spent on academic work in relation to other activities is shown in Chart I on page 87.

On the basis of a five-day week, full-time women students spend a slightly higher average amount of time on academic work than the full-time men students. The full-time women group spend on the average 8.2 hours a day in class and study from Monday through Friday. Full-time men students spend 8.1 hours.

Academic work is done on every day of the week. The average amount of time spent by students is, however, less on Saturday than from Monday to Friday and less on Sunday than on Saturday. Ninety per cent of the students who kept schedules study or attend classes or do both on Saturday. Sixty-two per cent study on Sunday. A higher percentage of full-time than of part-time students spend time on academic work on Saturday. The average amount of time spent by students who study on Sunday

TABLE XIII

AVERAGE NUMBER OF MINUTES SPENT IN CLASS AND STUDY BY 135 STUDENTS

GROUP	NO.	TIME SPENT					
		Av. No. of Minutes Spent per Point	Per Cent Over the 150 Minutes Required	Class or Study on Saturday		Study on Sunday	
				Number	%	Number	%
Full-Time Men							
Total	26	189	26	23	88	13	50
Having no degree ...	1	250	67	1	100	1	100
Having B.A. or B.S. .	16	173	15	14	87	8	50
Having M.A. or M.S.	9	204	36	8	89	4	44
Part-Time Men							
Total	15	277	85	13	86	10	67
Having no degree ...	0						
Having B.A. or B.S. .	4	232	55	3	75	2	50
Having M.A. or M.S.	11	296	97	10	91	8	73
Full-Time Women							
Total	59	186	24	57	97	46	78
Having no degree ...	14	187	25	14	100	12	86
Having B.A. or B.S. .	37	180	20	36	97	30	81
Having M.A. or M.S.	8	206	37	7	87	4	50
Part-Time Women							
Total	35	231	54	29	83	14	40
Having no degree ...	8	241	61	7	87	4	50
Having B.A. or B.S. .	18	166	11	15	83	5	27
Having M.A. or M.S.	9	422	182	7	78	6	67
Degrees							
Total	135	201	34	122	90	83	62
Having no degree ...	23	209	40	22	96	17	74
Having B.A. or B.S. .	75	180	20	68	91	44	59
Having M.A. or M.S.	37	285	90	32	87	22	59

is 4 hours. Fifty per cent of full-time men students spend on the average nearly 5 hours in study on Sunday. Seventy-eight per cent of full-time women students spend on the average 4.5 hours in study on Sunday.

Part-time students spend a larger average amount of time per point carried than full-time students. Full-time men students spend on an average 3.1 hours in class and study per academic point; part-time men students spend 4.6 hours. This difference is considerably reduced, however, when men who now hold the Master's degree are eliminated from both groups. The study time of full-time men students remains the same, but the study time of part-time men students is reduced to 3.8 hours. Since, however, the group of part-time men contains only four students, this difference has little significance.

Full-time women students average the same as the group of full-time men—3.1 hours, and part-time women students average 3.8 hours per point. The study time of both groups is the same (3.1 hours per point) when women holding the Master's degree are eliminated.

The entire group averages 3.3 hours in class and study for each point of academic work carried. The college catalogue states that 2.5 hours of class attendance and study are required for each point of work. The students who kept the schedules average 51 minutes more in study per point than the college catalogue requires. In other words, they are spending on the average nearly one more hour in preparation for each point of work than the requirement in the college catalogue.

The following figures indicate the distribution of students as to amount of time spent in study per point carried:

12 spend under 1 hour
16 spend from 1.0 to 1.4 hours
28 spend from 1.5 to 1.9 hours
26 spend from 2.0 to 2.4 hours
19 spend from 2.5 to 2.9 hours
12 spend from 3.0 to 3.4 hours
6 spend from 3.5 to 3.9 hours
4 spend from 4.0 to 4.4 hours
4 spend from 4.5 to 4.9 hours
8 spend over 5 hours

When the 37 students who now have the Master's degree and may be working for the Doctor's degree are eliminated from the distribution, the average amounts of time per point spent in study are as follows:

12 spend under 1 hour
11 spend from 1.0 to 1.4 hours
25 spend from 1.5 to 1.9 hours
21 spend from 2.0 to 2.4 hours
15 spend from 2.5 to 2.9 hours
9 spend from 3.0 to 3.4 hours
2 spend from 3.5 to 3.9 hours
0 spend from 4.0 to 4.4 hours
1 spends from 4.5 to 4.9 hours
2 spend over 5 hours

It is evident from the above distribution that one-half of the group of 98 students not working toward a Doctor's degree are spending 2 or more hours in preparation for each academic point.

4. *What Other Activities Are Encroaching on Leisure Time?* Chart I on page 87 indicates that students' time is taken up largely with four activities—sleeping, eating and personal care, academic work, and leisure. Another activity must be added to these four in the case of students who are working for remuneration.

It is of interest to note that full-time men students and part-time men students working for remuneration spend on the average approximately the same amount of time in leisure as the groups of men who are not working for remuneration. The activity which is reduced most in the daily schedule of men who work for remuneration is study.

Full-time women students do not spend so many hours on the average in work for remuneration as full-time men students; consequently their schedules are not influenced so much by this factor. The part-time women group not working for remuneration spend more time in household duties than any other group of women.

Religious activities and club, civic, and welfare activities consume a small portion of time on the average. Nearly all the religious activities of the students studied are on Sunday.

If the amount of leisure time is to be increased, academic work and work for remuneration appear to be the activities which should be lightened. Sleep, eating and personal duties, religious activities, and club and civic activities do not appear to be taking an undue amount of students' time.

5. *In What Recreational Activities Are Students Engaging?* Table XIV indicates the number of students who engaged in various leisure-time activities during the period in which the time schedules were kept. Chart II shows the percentage of leisure time devoted to each activity, and Chart III shows the percentage of men and of women participating in each activity.

The leisure-time activity most frequently recorded on students' schedules is informal sociability. Not only is this activity participated in by the largest number of students, but it occupies a larger amount of leisure time than any other activity. Women spend 22 per cent of their leisure time in this activity and men, 20 per cent.

Walking for recreation is reported by 124 students. Both men

TABLE XIV
KINDS OF LEISURE ACTIVITIES PARTICIPATED IN BY 135 STUDENTS DURING ONE WEEK

ACTIVITY	NUMBER	ACTIVITY	NUMBER
Informal Sociability	126	Theater	36
Visiting	116	Once	30
Bridge, cards	13	Twice	5
Play with children	2	Three times	1
Walking	124	Miscellaneous Recreation	34
		Recreation	19
Recreational Reading	115	Music	6
		Out for the evening	3
Rest	107	Leisure	2
Rest	68	Cross word puzzle	2
Nap, sleep	24	Play rehearsal	1
Relaxation	6	Entertainment	1
Loafing	5		
Sitting outside in the sun	3	Movies	30
Idle	2	Once	26
		Twice	4
Letter Writing	107		
		Sports and Games	30
Newspaper Reading	90	Swimming	7
Irregularly: 1–3 times	50	Volley ball	4
Regularly: 4–7 times	40	Football	4
		Hand ball	4
Formal Sociability	58	Bowling	4
Clubs, social affairs	23	Physical training	2
Dinners, teas, banquets	22	Ice skating	1
Parties, receptions	14	Tennis	1
Card parties	3	Tap dancing	1
Dances	2	Ping pong	1
		Golf	1
Lectures and Auditing Classes	55		
Once	37	Concert	21
Twice	13	Once	19
More than twice	5	Twice	1
		Three times	1
Trips	44		
Motoring	27	Opera	15
Trips	9	Once	14
Sight-seeing	4	Twice	1
Excursions	3		
Conventions	1	Museums and Exhibits	10
Radio	36	Spectator	10
		Football games	7
		Swimming meet	1
		Horse show	1
		Tennis	1

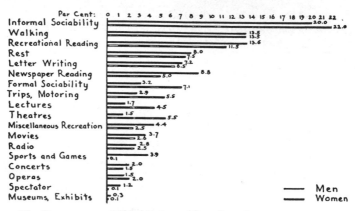

CHART II. Percentages of Total Leisure Time Devoted to Specific Activities by 135 Students (41 Men; 94 Women)

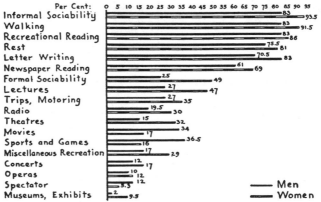

CHART III. Percentages of Men and Women Participating in Various Leisure Activities During One Week

and women spend 13.5 per cent of their leisure time in this activity. This is the only physical exercise reported by a large percentage of the group. According to the schedules, only 30 students participated in any game or sport. The difference between the men and women in this respect is noticeable. Thirty-seven per cent of the men in comparison with 16 per cent of the women participated in games and sports during the period in which the schedules were kept.

Recreational reading is third in the list of recreational activities both in the number of students who spend time on it and in the percentage of leisure time devoted to it. Eighty-three per cent of the men and 86 per cent of the women did some recreational reading during the week in which they kept the record of their activities.

Thirty-six students attended the theater, a higher number than attended the movies.

The time schedules indicate a decided lack of recreation involving physical exercise, particularly on the part of the women. The only physical exercise which is reported frequently is walking. Students spend about 30 minutes a day in this activity. Only 22 per cent engage in sports or games. Eighty-four per cent of the women's daily schedules show no physical exercise except walking. This lack of physical exercise seems a serious omission from the programs of students who spend a large amount of time in sedentary activities.

SUMMARY

1. Problems of leisure and recreation are second in frequency of problems reported in the Student Inquiry Blanks and are reported more frequently than any other problem in the student interviews. College officials are rarely consulted concerning problems of this nature, although a large percentage of students who have leisure problems are not solving them satisfactorily.

2. The specific problem stated by the large majority of students is lack of time for leisure.

3. In the interviews, over 50 per cent of students cited the pressure of academic work as the reason for their lack of leisure.

4. Student time schedules confirm the findings of the student interviews that few students are using the recreational facilities offered by the college, some because of lack of time and others because the facilities are not available at hours convenient for them.

5. Time schedules reveal the following facts regarding activities of students:

   a. Nine-tenths of the students' time from Monday to Friday is occupied with six activities: classes, study, eating and personal duties, sleeping, and leisure.

   b. Students spend approximately one-fourth of their waking time in leisure activities. They have on the average 3.2 hours of leisure from Monday to Friday, 5.4 hours on Saturday, and 6.4 hours on Sunday. The average for the week is 4 hours.

c. Full-time and part-time students spend approximately the same amount of time in leisure from Monday to Friday. Full-time students have more leisure on Saturday and part-time students, more on Sunday.

d. Working for remuneration tends to reduce the amount of time spent in academic work rather than the amount of leisure.

e. Students spend on the average 2.5 hours in preparation for each point of academic work. Fifty per cent of students not working for the Doctor's degree spend 2 or more hours in preparation per academic point.

f. Part-time students study on the average a larger amount of time per point than full-time students. When students now holding the Master's degree are eliminated, the differences are considerably reduced. The part-time men group still spend a larger amount of time per point than the full-time men group, but full-time and part-time women students spend the same amount.

g. Students devote time to academic work every day of the week. Ninety per cent of the students attend classes or study on Saturday and 62 per cent study on Sunday.

h. Walking is the only physical exercise in which a large percentage of the students engage. Only 37 per cent of the men and 16 per cent of the women take part in sports or games.

Chapter XI

OTHER PERSONAL PROBLEMS

THE five types of personal problems discussed in the preceding chapters make up 810 (63 per cent) of the 1,273 personal problems reported. The present chapter will deal with the personal problems less frequently mentioned, with the specific problems cited under each heading, with the consultations reported on these problems, and with the degree to which they have been solved. Although reported by fewer students than the problems previously discussed, the importance of many of the problems included in this chapter may be seen by a study of the specific problems mentioned. Problems reported by a comparatively small number of students are often more carefully stated than those cited more frequently. Because other types of problems were not reported, it cannot be assumed that they do not exist. The types of problems reported may be limited by the techniques used in the study.

LIVING CONDITIONS

Problems of living conditions are reported by 108 students. More full-time than part-time students cite problems in this area. Full-time women especially list problems of this type frequently. New students report difficulty with living conditions more often than former students; and single students, more frequently than married ones.

Specific Problems. The specific problems reported are:

	Number
Obtaining a place to live	26
Dissatisfied with furnishings of college apartments and dormitories	15
Present quarters not satisfactory	15
Finding place to live near the college	10
Dissatisfied with price of quarters	9
Irritating restrictions in college apartments and dormitories	7
Desire small unfurnished apartments	4

Dissatisfied with occupants of living quarters 4
Living quarters too dark 3
No place to practice music 3
Finding living quarters in more desirable
  neighborhood 2
Live in dormitory or in private apartment? 2
Dissatisfied with dormitory dining rooms 1
What proportion of money to spend on apart-
  ment? 1
Maids should enter dormitory rooms daily 1
City noises in college halls 1
College halls and cafeteria too expensive 1
Finding good place in which to eat 1
Part-time student would like to live in col-
  lege dormitory 1

Consultation Regarding Problems. Forty-seven of the 108 students reporting problems of living conditions have consulted some college official regarding them. Fifty-nine conferences are reported with the following officials:

	Number
College Business Office	17
Welfare Director	11
Professors	11
Social Directors of Dormitories	8
University Business Office	5
Others	7

It is evident that various agencies are consulted on these problems. Seventy-two per cent of the conferences are considered helpful.

Degree to Which Problems Have Been Solved. Since one's living quarters are an important factor in one's general health and happiness, it is of interest to see how successfully students are solving their problems of this type. The degrees to which students have been able to solve them are:

	Number	Per Cent
Satisfactorily solved	50	46.3
Partially solved	11	10.2
Unsolved or unsatisfactorily solved	30	27.8
No solution indicated	17	15.7

PHYSICAL HEALTH

Problems of physical health are reported by 92 students. The proportion of problems of this type increases in each age group.

These problems are reported by students as follows:

> 3.8 per cent of students under 25
> 9.9 per cent of students from 25 to 34
> 10.0 per cent of students from 35 to 44
> 13.7 per cent of students 45 and over

These problems are cited by the same percentage of married and of single students and of men and of women. They are reported most frequently by the "unsigned" group of full-time students.

Specific Problems.   Students report the following specific health problems:

	Number
Physical health	38
Eyes	7
Medical care for family	6
Where find a dentist charging moderate rates?	4
Lack physical strength	3
Obtaining physical examination	3
Indigestion	3
Headaches	2
Colds	2
Nervous exhaustion	2
Where to obtain hemoglobin test	2
Insomnia	2
Emergency illness	2
Health poor on account of lack of physical exercise	2
Continue in school or have operation?	2
Ptomaine poisoning	1
Sprained ankle	1
Heart trouble	1
Difficulty in adjusting diet	1
Health problems arising from crowded, poorly ventilated classrooms	1
Where find a doctor charging moderate rates?	1
Hearing affected	1
Recuperating from operation	1
Sinus trouble	1
Nervous breakdown	1
Where obtain hay fever inoculation?	1
Poor health due to carrying too heavy a schedule	1

Consultation Regarding Problems.   Fifty-four students (59 per cent) have consulted college officials concerning their health problems as follows:

	Number
College physician	32
Professors	14
Welfare Director	12
Physicians outside college	5
Others	5

Eighty-nine per cent of the conferences on health problems are reported as helpful.

Degree to Which Problems Have Been Solved. Health problems are reported solved to the following extent:

	Number	Per Cent
Satisfactorily solved	42	45.7
Partially solved	23	25.0
Unsatisfactorily solved	6	6.5
Unsolved	12	13.0
No solution indicated	9	9.8

TIME DISTRIBUTION

Specific Problems. Time distribution presents a problem to 75 students. It is a problem especially to full-time women students and to new students. All problems of this type relate to the budgeting of time. Part-time students cite problems of conflicting demands of their positions, their academic work, their home duties, and their recreation. Full-time students report problems of accomplishing their academic work and having time left for recreation. Those who are working part-time must try to maintain a balance between their academic work, work for remuneration, and leisure time. The following are examples of problems mentioned:

How can I do my regular teaching, take courses, and still secure needed leisure?

How shall I organize my time and work in order to make sure I have the proper amount of recreation?

How can I teach full-time, study part-time, and keep house in 24 hours a day?

How can I arrange to do my studying and still keep well and have some time for recreation?

How can I systematize my work to save time?

Consultation Regarding Problems. Only 9 students of the 75 reporting problems of time distribution have consulted a college official concerning them. All but one of those consulted are professors, and all conferences but one are considered helpful.

Degree to Which Problems Have Been Solved. Students report their problems in this field solved to the following degrees:

	Number	Per Cent
Satisfactorily solved	11	14.7
Partially solved	26	34.6
Unsatisfactorily solved	4	5.3
Unsolved	15	20.0
No solution indicated	19	25.0

Eight of the 11 who have solved their problems satisfactorily state that they have done so through working out time budgets. Those who have reached unsatisfactory solutions state that they are depriving themselves of sleep and recreation, are neglecting courses and friends, and have had to cut classes.

PROFESSIONAL PROBLEMS

Specific Problems. Professional problems are of many different kinds, as may be seen by the accompanying list. It will be noted that many may be considered "constructive problems."

	Number
Considering change of profession	12
Considering change of position	6
Teach or continue studies?	5
Finish degree or accept offer of a good position?	4
How obtain additional training?	3
Attend college or travel?	2
How best spend my one year in professional school on a limited income	2
Take full-time position and study summers or carry part-time position and study along with it?	2
Shall I take Saturday classes or go to summer school?	2
How much college work shall I carry while teaching full-time?	1
Organization of department in a school	1
Shall I accept position while working on dissertation?	1
Shall I work for doctorate and do part-time work?	1
Which educational field shall I enter?	1
How shall I integrate my work with my study?	1
Advancing age a professional handicap	1
Accept position with good salary and not many other advantages or one with small salary and good experience?	
Shall I prepare for the high school or college field?	11

How improve public school standards of work?   1
Shall I become a teacher or a research worker?   1

Consultation Regarding Problems. Students consult college officials frequently on problems of this kind. Twenty-two of the 49 students reporting problems of this nature have consulted some college official. Ninety per cent of consultations have been with professors. All conferences on this problem are reported helpful.

Degree to Which Problems Have Been Solved. Students report their problems as being solved as follows:

	Number	Per Cent
Satisfactorily solved	24	49.0
Unsolved	18	36.7
No solution indicated	7	14.3

MENTAL HEALTH

Specific Problems. Problems of mental health are cited by the same percentage of men and of women. Of the 224 students under 25 years of age, only one cites a problem of mental health. The specific problems reported are:

	Number
Emotional adjustment	21
Mental health	8
Worry over academic standing	8
Inferiority complex	4
Discouragement	2
Worry over financial matters	2
Worry over the future	1
Worry over possible illness	1
Worry over securing a position because of barrier of marriage	1
Nervousness in class	1

Problems of emotional adjustment make up 43 per cent of those in this category. Worry over academic standing accounts for one-sixth of all problems of this type.

Consultation Regarding Problems. Only 11 students of the 49 who report mental health problems have consulted any college official concerning them. These 11 students have had 17 conferences. Ten are reported with professors, 3 with the college physician, and 4 with other officials.

Degree to Which Problems Have Been Solved. Students are endeavoring to solve their problems of mental health in the following ways:

> Am limiting my academic schedule
> Have sought professional assistance
> Am under care of a physician
> Am taking more time for social life
> Have registered in a physical education class
> Am trying to solve it through work
> Am trying to forget about it

Four students have been able to solve their problems of mental health satisfactorily. The problems are reported solved to the following extent:

	Number	Per Cent
Satisfactorily solved	4	8.2
Partially solved	17	34.7
Unsolved	14	28.6
No solution indicated	14	28.6

HOME CONDITIONS

Specific Problems. Twenty-seven students cite problems of home conditions. Married students mention them more frequently than single students. The specific problems reported are:

	Number
Family problems	7
Responsibility to financially dependent parents	5
Separation from family	4
Placement of children while working	3
Adjustment to death in family	2
Maintain home and do creditable work in studies	1
Unhappy home life	1
Domestic difficulties threaten professional future	1
How much to accede to emotional demands made by mother	1
Care of sick in home while working full-time	1
Adjustment of home life to college demands	1

Consultation Regarding Problems. Six students report conferences concerning problems of this type. Five conferences are reported with professors and one with the Welfare Director. Five of the 6 consultations were considered helpful.

Degree to Which Problems Have Been Solved. Solutions reported fall into the following groupings:

	Number	Per Cent
Satisfactorily solved	3	11.1
Partially solved	10	37.1
Unsolved	8	29.6
No solution indicated	6	22.2

RELIGION AND PHILOSOPHY OF LIFE

Specific Problems. Although only 18 students cite religious problems, it will be seen from the accompanying list that a number of the problems are critical to the students who report them. Specific problems listed are:

	Number
Adjusting religious beliefs to new ideas	8
Affiliation with church	1
Loss of faith in prayer	1
What do I believe about God?	1
How can I learn to believe in the doctrines of church and in a personal deity?	1
Will my viewpoint of religion change as others have changed?	1
Shall I carry over denying religion and changing name for sake of "expediency"? (Jewish student)	1
How can I accept pragmatism without giving up my religion?	1
Where to go to church	1
Teach Sunday School or attend various churches?	1
Religious difficulty	1

From the interviews, four kinds of religious problems may be distinguished:

1. Those involving a loss of faith in beliefs previously held and in some cases a renunciation of the church in which the student was reared.

2. Those arising usually from the student's lack of religious training in youth and resulting in a feeling of desiring and needing a religion of some kind.

3. Those arising from difficulty with colleagues because of holding more liberal ideas than they. This type of problem was cited several times by returned missionaries.

4. Those caused by a conflict between religious ideas and scientific theory.

Consultation Regarding Problems.   Only 3 students have consulted anyone officially connected with the college concerning their religious problems.   The officers consulted were professors in each case.   The 3 conferences are reported as having been helpful in solving the problems.   Two of the consultations were concerning the adjustment of religious beliefs to new ideas and one, the question of a personal God.

Degree to Which Problems Have Been Solved.   Students report that they are trying to solve their religious difficulties by:

Trying to learn tolerance.
Taking courses in religion.
Keeping an open mind.
Working in the church.
Reading and discussing problem with a friend.
Giving up position.

The serious nature of some of the problems may be seen in the instance of one student, a religious worker, who states that she has lost faith in prayer and has given up her position as a result.

Religious problems have been solved to the following degrees:

	Number	Per Cent
Satisfactorily solved	0	0.0
Partially solved	11	55.5
Unsolved	6	39.0
No solution indicated	1	5.5

ADJUSTMENT TO PHYSICAL ENVIRONMENT

Specific Problems.   Problems relating to adjustment to the physical environment are largely brought about by the complexity of life in a large city.   Problems reported are:

	Number
Adjustment to city life	6
Crowded conditions	3
Dislike for city life	2
Difficulty in getting around city	1
Traffic noises	1
Adjustment of foreign student to new environment	1

Consultation.   Only one consultation is reported on problems of this type.   A foreign student having difficulty in adjusting to new conditions reports having conferred with a professor concerning the difficulty. She considered the conference helpful.

Degree to Which Problems Have Been Solved. Students have solved problems of this nature to the following extent:

	Number	Per Cent
Satisfactorily solved	0	0.0
Partially solved	6	42.9
Unsolved	3	21.4
No solution indicated	5	35.7

PERSONALITY PROBLEMS

Specific Problems. Eight women, 5 men, and 1 anonymous student cite problems of personality such as the following:

	Number
Lack of personal initiative	6
Poor social adjustment	3
Self-consciousness	2
Feel odd in present style of clothes	2
How may I improve my personality?	1

Consultation. Of the 3 consultations reported, 2 were with personnel officers and 1 with a professor. All were considered helpful.

Degree to Which Problems Have Been Solved. Problems of this type have been solved in the following degree:

	Number	Per Cent
Satisfactorily solved	0	0.0
Partially solved	2	14.2
Unsolved	6	42.9
No solution indicated	6	42.9

MISCELLANEOUS PROBLEMS

Specific Problems. Problems classed as miscellaneous include the following:

	Number
How can I satisfy my desire to know more?	3
Gaining cooperation of faculty in regard to student activities	2
Where to shop quickly and satisfactorily	2
Securing publisher and criticism for book	2
Shall I dress beyond my means to keep up appearance?	1
How much life insurance shall I carry and what kind?	1

Where to store car	1
Immigration laws confront foreign students	1
How to help a friend adjust herself	1
How may a teacher agitate for changes in the educational system?	1
Finding someone to rent apartment for summer	1
Finding time for chapel	1

Consultation. Five conferences are reported on these problems; all were with professors. Three are reported as helpful, one as not helpful, and on one no report is given.

Degree to Which Problems Have Been Solved. Miscellaneous problems have been solved in the following degrees:

	Number	Per Cent
Satisfactorily solved	4	23.5
Partially solved	2	11.8
Unsolved	6	35.3
No solution indicated	5	29.4

SUMMARY

The ten problems included in this chapter make up 37 per cent of the total number of personal problems. Although reported comparatively seldom, some of the problems are of a serious nature and are of considerable importance to the students who mention them.

Problems regarding physical health, living conditions, professional matters, and mental health are brought in largest numbers for consultation to some officer of the college.

Professors are consulted on every type of problem.

Problems of living conditions, physical health, and professional matters are reported as having been satisfactorily solved more frequently than other problems.

Chapter XII

THE COMPLEXITY OF PROBLEMS

Up to the present point, the problems and the groups wherein they are found have been the units of consideration. Each problem has been studied from the standpoint of the frequency with which it is reported, the specific kinds of problems mentioned, the consultations reported, and the solutions indicated. Problems reported most frequently have been dealt with in some detail. Various student groups have been studied with regard to the problems reported most frequently, problems reported by a larger percentage of one group than another, and the average number of problems per person reported in each group. The unit of consideration in the present chapter is the individual. The chapter deals with patterns of problems frequently found in individuals of the interview group.

PATTERNS OF PROBLEMS IN THE STUDENT INTERVIEW GROUP

Problems do not often occur singly. They are associated with one another and the existence of one problem in an individual may aggravate the conditions of other problems. To use Strang's illustration:

> Problems appear layer upon layer like the skins of an onion. When one is removed, another is disclosed, going deeper and deeper until real motives and origins are reached.[1]

Individuals of the interview group were studied to ascertain the patterns of problems most frequently found. For example, how many students have problems of finance and placement associated together? How many have these and additional problems? Various problem patterns which occur frequently are shown in the paragraphs that follow:

Frequent Combinations of Problems Involving Finance. The

[1] Ruth Strang, "Personal Problems of Students", p. 151. Proceedings of the National Association of Deans of Women, Washington, D. C., Association. 1929.

following patterns of problems are found among the 125 students who report finance as a problem:

	Number
Finance and placement	91
Finance and leisure	82
Finance and part-time work	60
Finance, placement, and leisure	53
Finance, placement, leisure, and social relationships	32
Finance, placement, leisure, social relationships, and part-time work	17

Frequent Combinations of Problems Involving Part-Time Work. Eighty-five students with problems of part-time work have the following combinations of problems:

	Number
Part-time work and finance	60
Part-time work and placement	59
Part-time work, finance, and placement	47
Part-time work, leisure, social relationships, and finance	24
Part-time work, social relationships, finance, and placement	20

Frequent Combinations of Problems Involving Placement. Patterns of problems of the 126 students with placement problems are:

	Number
Placement and finance	91
Placement and part-time work	59
Placement, finance, and leisure	53
Placement, finance, and part-time work	47
Placement, finance, leisure, and social relationships	32
Placement, finance, social relationships, and part-time work	20

Frequent Combinations of Problems Involving Social Relationships. The 110 students with problems of social relationships have the following combinations of problems:

	Number
Social relationships and leisure	80
Social relationships and part-time work	45
Social relationships, leisure, and finance	45
Social relationships, leisure, finance, and part-time work	24
Social relationships, leisure, and time distribution	16

Frequent Combinations of Problems Involving Leisure. Frequent problem patterns of the 133 students who have problems of leisure and recreation are:

	Number
Leisure and finance	82
Leisure and social relationships	80
Leisure and part-time work	53
Leisure, finance, and social relationships	45
Leisure, social relationships, and time distribution	45
Leisure, finance, part-time work, and social relationships	24

"BASIC" AND ASSOCIATED PROBLEMS IN THE STUDENT INTERVIEW GROUP

The preceding section has dealt with the patterns of problems found in individuals of the interview group. Not only are problems frequently associated with one another, but in many cases one problem appears to be the immediate cause of other problems. For example, the lack of money may give rise to problems of part-time work and recreation.

The information concerning each student was studied by the interviewer in an effort to determine whether one personal problem might be considered the "basic" problem of that student. Information was available from the Student Inquiry Blanks as to which problem the student considered most important. The interviews also often revealed the problem which seemed to be at the heart of the difficulty. From these two sources of information, the interviewer judged the basic nature of the problems. The interpretation of the basic nature of the problem by a psychologist or psychiatrist would doubtless have been different, reaching down perhaps to deeper levels of the individual's personality, but as far as the interviewer was able to go, certain problems seemed to underlie other problems, and these for want of a better term have been designated "basic" problems.

Two students have no important problems as far as could be discovered; the fundamental problems of three students are academic. The basic and associated problems of the remaining 210 students are shown in Table XV. The following statements, taken from this table, as to the number of students to whom any problem is "basic" should be understood as meaning, "basic in the interpretation of the interviewer."

TABLE XV

ASSOCIATION OF PERSONAL PROBLEMS IN INDIVIDUALS OF THE INTERVIEW GROUP

BASIC PROBLEM	FRE-QUEN-CY	ASSOCIATED PROBLEMS														
		1*	2*	3*	4*	5*	6*	7*	8*	9*	10*	11*	12*	13*	14*	15*
1. Finance	69		46	49	29	32	9	8	14	0	5	1	4	1	4	5
2. Placement	35	21		15	17	20	2	7	8	0	1	0	1	0	4	1
3. Leisure	21	4	10		14	3	1	2	2	0	0	1	0	1	0	0
4. Social relationships ...	16	4	8	9		4	5	2	2	0	1	0	0	0	1	0
5. Part-time work	15	5	5	11	7		3	1	4	0	1	0	0	0	2	0
6. Time distribution	12	5	4	9	7	4		5	2	0	0	1	0	0	2	1
7. Physical health	11	6	4	4	5	0	2		0	1	2	0	0	0	3	0
8. Living conditions	8	1	1	0	3	2	0	0		0	0	0	0	0	0	0
9. Religion	8	4	8	6	5	3	0	1	2		1	0	1	1	1	1
10. Mental health	5	3	4	5	3	0	1	0	0	0		1	0	0	1	0
11. Physical environment ..	5	1	0	2	3	2	1	3	2	0	0		1	0	1	0
12. Home conditions	5	2	1	2	1	0	1	1	0	0	0	0		0	2	0
13. Personality	0															
14. Professional problems	0															
15. Miscellaneous	0															
Total	210	56	91	112	94	70	25	30	36	1	11	3	8	3	21	8

*Indicates classification corresponding to the same number in the vertical column at the left.

This table should be read: Finance is a basic problem to 69 students; it is associated with problems of placement 46 times, leisure, 49 times, etc.

Finance is the immediate basic problem with 69 students. Problems associated most frequently with those of finance are placement, leisure and recreation, part-time work, and social relationships.

An illustration of a student with serious financial problems is that of a woman over forty, unmarried, and studying for the Doctor's degree. During her earning period she has been the support of mother, father, and a crippled boy. The drain on her resources from these dependents prevented her from saving when teaching. She felt that she had reached the limit of possible advancement in the field in which she was working and determined to return to school at any cost. Since she began work at the college she has borrowed on her insurance policy, from the college, and from a foundation, through the assistance of one of her professors. At times she has lacked funds to meet the bills for the ensuing week. At the beginning of the current semester she had no definite idea of how she would or could meet her expenses. She has now borrowed a sufficient amount to support herself for the remainder of the academic year. When she finishes the school year, she will be about $2,000 in debt.

Worry over her financial situation has involved problems of mental as well as physical health. Her recreational opportunities have been limited by her physical condition, by the necessity of carrying a heavy academic schedule in order to finish as quickly as possible, and by lack of money for entertainment. Opportunity for social contacts has been restricted by lack of a reception room for guests. Her problem is one of having begun graduate study under a financial handicap so severe that it has affected adversely her physical condition and her academic, social, and recreational activities.

Placement seems to be the fundamental problem with 35 students and is most frequently associated with finance, leisure and recreation, part-time work, and social relationships.

The following cases illustrate the complexity of placement problems. A colored girl, single, between the ages of 30 and 35, with 10 years' teaching experience, a new student in the college, lost her position last spring. Failing to obtain another position, she came to school. She had not expected to study this year and had little money to meet her expenses. She planned to do part-time work while in college, but up to the present has secured only intermittent serving jobs. She prepares all her own meals, keeping the cost within twenty to thirty cents a day. The time, however, which is required for marketing and the preparation of the meals robs her of time she would like to have for study. She has neither time nor money for making social contacts or for recreation. When she entered school she shifted to a new major field and feels very uncertain of the opportunities for her in the new work.

Her problems appear to fall into the following sequence: basic problem—loss of position, resulting in financial stress; this in turn causes difficulties in the fields of leisure and recreation and social relationships.

Another example of a placement problem is that of a young man 25 years old, who was married during the past summer. He has had no teaching experience. He began graduate study immediately after finishing his undergraduate work. He now has the Master's degree, but has not been able to secure a position. He is relying for support on his wife, who is working part-time. His failure to obtain placement has brought financial trouble and also the problem of obtaining some kind of part-time work, if no full-time work is forthcoming. Although he was born in this country, his name is foreign. Fearing that his name may be a hindrance to obtaining a position, he is asking the courts to permit him to use an American name. His basic problem, that of securing vocational placement, is further complicated by lack of experience in teaching. The failure to obtain a position is the more serious because of a previously incurred debt and the financial dependence of parents. The problem now evolves into one of finding part-time work. Although he has leisure time in abundance, the problem of placement so occupies his thoughts that he does not use his leisure time to advantage.

The question of *leisure and recreation*, although a problem to 133 students, was characterized by the interviewer as basic in only 21 cases. Problems of this nature are usually a result of other factors. They are most often associated with problems of social relationships and placement.

An illustration of a case where a student regards leisure as her fundamental problem is that of a woman who is working for the Doctor's degree. She feels that a very fundamental need of students is to develop interests other than the strictly vocational. She believes that students rush too hard and too fast and do not take time enough to develop cultural interests. Her own hobby is painting, but she has not had time to cultivate it since she began work toward the Doctor's degree.

Another example is that of a man formerly in the physical education department of a large university who is at present studying for the Doctor's degree. He is earning enough to support his wife and himself by part-time work and is working on his dissertation. His chief form of recreation before beginning graduate study was tennis. He has no time to play now. Being accustomed to physical exercise, he feels the lack of it keenly.

The problem of *social relationships* appears to be basic to 16 students and is associated most frequently with problems of leisure and placement. The way in which it operates as a basic problem may be seen in the case of a woman over 45 years of age who is working for the Doctor's degree. She has saved money enough to meet her expenses; consequently she has no problems of finance or part-time work. She is able to pay for adequate living quarters. She is on leave of absence and has no placement problem. She feels very much alone, however, and has few social contacts which are satisfying to her. She would like opportunity to meet people with interests similar to her own. Her only social contacts thus far have been those opened through a church club which she attends. Her problem of lack of a companion and friends involves also the matter of her leisure and recreation.

Part-time work is a fundamental problem to 15 students and is associated most frequently with problems of leisure, social relationships, and finance.

The following illustration indicates the problems arising in connection with part-time work. A young man under 25 years of age, married, has held a part-time position paying $150 a month and requiring five hours' work a day. He is carrying eighteen points of academic work. The strain of the academic work and his part-time position have exhausted him physically. The day before the interview he lost his part-time position. He had been using the money earned to repay a school debt. He is now worn out physically, with academic work to make up, with no money, and faced with the necessity of securing immediate employment of some kind or of asking for an additional loan from the college.

Another type of part-time work problem is that of a girl who prefers the work which she is doing in a fashionable restaurant to her academic work and is constantly pressed for time in her school work because of the time spent in her part-time work, for which she receives a very small remuneration.

Time distribution is most frequently associated with leisure and social relationships. The reason it is a fundamental problem to some students is seen in the case of a woman over forty who is married and has two children. She carries sixteen points at the college, teaches two days a week in a junior high school, takes care of a twelve-room house, plans the meals for her family, and has charge of a department in the church school. It is easy to see why time distribution is a problem to her.

Physical health is a problem to 41 students of the interview group and is considered basic in over one-fourth of the cases in which it was disclosed. It is most commonly associated with problems of finance, social relationships, leisure, and placement.

A striking illustration of a case in which health is the basic problem is that of a girl 23 years old who is having such serious eye trouble that she is considering dropping the sixteen points for which she is registered. This health problem is further complicated by her feeling of responsibility to the institution which granted her a scholarship of $200 for graduate work. The institution wishes her to continue her study even though she loses academic credit.

Another illustration of the way in which a basic health problem has affected other relationships is found in the case of a student whose hearing is seriously impaired. This physical defect has resulted in the loss of her position and in the changing of her major from religious education to speech. It has interfered with normal social relationships, and has required a difficult emotional as well as vocational adjustment.

The train of consequences resulting from a major health difficulty is illustrated in the case of a woman student between 25 and 34 years of age who should have a serious operation. Finance is involved because the student is unable to pay for the operation; recreation is involved because she lacks energy for physical activity and social participation; and academic work is necessarily affected adversely. Failure to secure the Master's degree toward which she is working may result in a serious placement problem, since it is necessary for her to obtain the degree in order to retain the position from which she is now on leave of absence. Mental health problems result from worry over all these difficulties.

Living conditions are classified as the basic problems of only 8 students. The problem is usually that of living at such a distance from the college that considerable time must be spent in commuting.

Nine students interviewed spoke of *religious difficulties*. In 8 of these 9 instances, religion is regarded as the fundamental problem. It is most frequently associated with problems of placement, recreation, and social relationships.

The manner in which religious problems may cause difficulty in other areas is seen in the case of a young man under 25 years of age who is just beginning graduate study. When he began his college work his family gave him no encouragement and no financial assistance. During his college career he lived with a family whose religious beliefs were different from those of his own family. They were very kind to him and made it possible for him to stay in college. His social contacts were with people of their faith. He now wishes to become a member of the church to which his friends belong but is having some difficulty in gaining his own intellectual consent. He also fears that the change may affect his chances of obtaining a position. He realizes also that it will cause a serious break with his own family. His problem seems to be that of desiring to become a member of a religious group much different from that of his early training as a token of gratitude to his friends. He believes that the new faith will not satisfy him intellectually, may affect adversely his chances of obtaining a position, and may cause a break with his family. Shall he or shall he not take the step he is considering?

Another man, a native of Austria, over 35 years of age, has broken away from the religious faith which he held earlier. He has been pastor of large churches here and abroad. His friends disapprove of his breaking away from the church. He feels that he has lost his old friends and has not made new ones. He has been very lonely. It is now necessary for him to obtain work in a new field. He has almost no money. He does his own cooking in order to reduce expenses. He is worried over the future and is despondent. The break from the religious faith in which he was reared has brought about for this man serious problems of placement, social relationships, and finance. The lack of friends and of money has created problems of leisure and recreation. His physical and mental health has been impaired by worry over his situation.

Mental health, adjustment to physical environment, and *home conditions* were classified as immediate basic problems in five cases each.

Two examples of mental health problems illustrate the nature of a number of problems of this classification. A woman 28 years of age has been out of school work of any kind for four years. She worries about her examinations and about whether she is getting as much as she should from her courses to such an extent that her general efficiency is impaired.

Another woman who is between 25 and 34 years of age worries about her academic work to such an extent that she cannot sleep. She has been taking a daily walk and reading light literature before trying to go to sleep, but cannot get her mind off the problems of the day. Worry and loss of sleep complicate the problem of her academic work.

Problems of adjustment to physical environment are often fundamental to foreign students who find it difficult to adjust to different climatic conditions, food to which they are unaccustomed, and the general hurry and bustle of a large city. An illustration of difficulties of this kind is the case of a woman 28 years of age, a native of Armenia. When she came to this country she lacked courage to consult a physician regarding matters of diet or to confer with someone who could have helped her adjust to the new conditions. As a result of having to make too many adjustments in a short space of time she had a physical and nervous breakdown and was forced to give up her work and go to the country for a rest.

The serious nature of problems of home conditions is apparent in the case of a woman of 30 who is married and has one child. Her husband is tired of home responsibilities and wants to get away. He has agreed, however, to continue to help support the family until his wife can get her degree and support herself and the child. It is a question from day to day how long the family can hold together. At present the woman is carrying her home responsibilities, caring for the child, and taking 10 points of academic work, hoping to be able to get a degree and a position in the near future.

The illustrations cited, although typical of the kinds of problems revealed in the interviews, may give an exaggerated picture of the acuteness of the problems of the group in general. They represent the outstanding cases of difficulties which were found in various areas of adjustment.

In contrast to these instances of students who have not been able to solve their problems successfully, it is of interest to consider one who has achieved what appears to be a well-balanced schedule. This student, a woman between 25 and 34 years of age, is working for the Doctor's degree. She has two part-time positions in the college, one as assistant and one as a part-time instructor, which enable her to meet her expenses comfortably. She has planned her leisure and recreation as carefully as her academic work. She plans to swim once in two weeks, often spends a week-end in the country, attends the theater once a week regardless of how much work she has, and reads two novels a week. She plans to have either a dinner or an informal tea in her apartment once a week and invites not only old friends but people whom she has met and with whom she would like to become better acquainted. She attends the Graduate Club in order to enlarge her circle of acquaintances in the college. She appears to be master of her work, rather than mastered by it.

SUMMARY

This chapter has dealt with the patterns of problems frequently found in individuals of the interview group, with their underlying and associated problems, and with examples of some of the underlying problems. The following are facts worth noting.

1. Problems of finance, part-time work, placement, social relationships, and leisure not only occur frequently within the group but are often associated with one another.

2. The following combinations are frequently found:

Finance and placement.
Finance and part-time work.
Finance and leisure.
Finance, placement, and leisure.
Finance, leisure, and social relationships.

Part-time work and placement.
Part-time work and social relationships.
Part-time work and leisure.
Part-time work, placement, and finance.

Social relationships and leisure.
Social relationships, leisure, and time distribution.

3. Finance is the basic problem to the largest number of students—69. Placement is second, being the fundamental problem of 35 students.

4. Although religious problems are reported only 9 times, they are regarded as basic in 8 of the 9 instances.

Chapter XIII

THE PROCESS OF PROBLEM SOLUTION

The preceding chapters have dealt with the types of problems stated by students, the factors associated with the problems most frequently mentioned, and with the degree to which students report that their problems have been solved. The present chapter is concerned in general with the process of problem solution and in particular with the rôle of personnel officers and professors in the solution of student problems.

TYPES OF PROBLEMS BROUGHT FOR CONSULTATION TO COLLEGE OFFICIALS

According to their reports, students are more inclined to consult college officials regarding their academic problems than regarding their personal problems. Tables XVI and XVII show that 35 per cent of all personal problems in comparison with 56 per cent of academic problems reported were brought to college officers for consultation.

There is a wide variation in the percentage of consultations on various types of personal and academic problems. Of the former group, a relatively high percentage of part-time work, physical health, living conditions, placement, and professional problems are brought for consultation to officials of the college. Finance, mental health, home conditions, personality and miscellaneous problems are in the middle group in percentage of consultation. A small percentage of problems of religion, adjustment to the physical environment, time distribution, leisure, and social relationships come to college officers for conference. Of the academic problems, the highest percentages of consultations are regarding difficulties relating to courses, degrees, and general problems of advisement. Study, personal and professional development, and miscellaneous problems are in the center group in percentage of consultation. The lowest group comprises problems of academic standing, lacks in the physical environment, and lacks in the student's training.

1. *Problems Regarding Which Professors Are Consulted As Reported by Students.* The important rôle of the faculty in counseling students is indicated both in Table XVI and in Table XVII. Seventy per cent of the 1,664 conferences reported are with professors.

Although members of the faculty are consulted frequently concerning both personal and academic problems, their major counseling function is in regard to *academic* problems. Eighty-four per cent of all conferences reported on academic problems are with professors. Of the 1,182 conferences with professors, 932 concern academic problems. Eighty per cent of the conferences on problems of this type are regarding courses and degrees. Over 90 per cent of the conferences on courses concern getting desired courses, choice of courses, and choice of major. The conferences regarding degrees deal with requirements for a degree and the question of whether to work for a degree. Almost three-fourths of the confer-

TABLE XVI

PROPORTIONS OF PERSONAL PROBLEMS BROUGHT FOR CONSULTATION TO SOME OFFICER OF THE COLLEGE

PROBLEM	CONSULTATION				PERSON CONSULTED				WAS CONFERENCE HELPFUL?			
	Yes		No		Professor		Others		Yes		No	
	No.	%	No.	%	No.	%	No.	%	No.	%	No.	%
Finance	80	36.2	141	63.8	42	40.8	61	59.2	65	86.7	10	13.3
Leisure	19	12.3	136	87.7	11	51.5	10	49.5	12	85.7	2	14.3
Part-time work .	102	67.1	50	32.9	43	38.0	70	62.0	73	70.8	30	29.2
Placement	66	44.0	84	56.0	56	55.5	45	44.5	43	65.2	23	34.8
Social relationships	12	9.1	120	90.9	5	38.5	8	61.5	7	88.0	1	12.0
Living conditions	47	43.5	61	56.5	11	19.0	47	81.0	41	72.0	16	28.0
Physical health .	54	58.7	38	41.3	14	22.3	49	77.4	56	88.9	7	11.1
Time distribution	9	12.0	66	88.0	6	85.7	1	14.3	6	85.7	1	14.3
Professional problems	22	44.9	27	55.1	37	90.2	4	9.8	41	100.0	0	0.0
Mental health ..	11	22.5	38	77.5	10	62.5	6	37.5	14	82.4	3	17.6
Home conditions	6	22.2	21	77.8	5	83.3	1	16.7	5	83.8	1	16.7
Religion	3	16.7	15	83.4	3	100.0	0	0.0	3	100.0	0	0.0
Miscellaneous ...	5	29.4	12	70.6	5	100.0	0	0.0	3	75.0	1	25.0
Physical environment	1	7.1	13	92.9	1	100.0	0	0.0	1	100.0	0	0.0
Personality problems	3	21.4	11	78.6	1	33.3	2	66.7	3	100.0	0	0.0
Total	440	34.5	833	65.5	250	45.2	304	54.8	373	79.7	95	20.3

TABLE XVII

PROPORTIONS OF ACADEMIC PROBLEMS BROUGHT FOR CONSULTATION TO SOME OFFICER OF THE COLLEGE

PROBLEMS PERTAINING TO	CONSULTATION				PERSON CONSULTED				WAS CONFERENCE HELPFUL?			
	Yes		No		Professor		Others		Yes		No	
	No.	%	No.	%	No.	%	No.	%	No.	%	No.	%
Courses	389	60.8	250	39.2	478	92.3	40	7.7	419	85.4	72	14.6
Degrees and certificates	248	69.5	109	30.5	280	79.1	74	20.9	272	84.5	50	15.5
Study	63	33.5	125	66.5	14	21.8	50	78.2	31	51.7	29	48.3
General advisement	71	71.0	29	29.0	73	90.1	8	9.9	55	67.9	26	32.1
Personal and professional development	37	50.0	37	50.0	46	97.9	1	2.1	45	95.7	2	4.3
Academic standing	15	23.0	50	77.0	17	94.5	1	5.5	13	72.2	5	27.8
Lacks in physical environment ..	7	17.9	32	82.1	8	88.9	1	11.1	4	57.2	3	42.8
Lacks in Student's training	7	24.1	22	75.9	7	87.5	1	12.5	6	75.0	2	25.0
Miscellaneous ...	7	26.9	19	73.1	9	81.6	2	18.4	11	100.0	0	0.0
Total	844	55.6	673	44.4	932	84.0	178	16.0	856	81.9	189	18.1

ences on personal problems are concerning finance, part-time work, placement, and professional matters.

As Shown by Professors' Records of Student Interviews. The 88 interview records kept by 7 professors for a brief period of time cannot, of course, give an adequate picture of the work with individual students which is being done by the faculty as a whole. They do, however, indicate the types of problems concerning which professors are being consulted.

The interview records corroborate students' reports with regard to the important rôle of the faculty in counseling on academic problems. Fifty-three of the 88 interviews deal with academic problems. The problems of this type which were reported in the interviews with a frequency of two or more are:

	Number
Orientation	7
Requirements for degree	5
Choice of major	3
Securing materials for study	3
Selection of a dissertation topic	2

The personal problems concerning which professors interviewed students, during the period in which the records were kept, are:

	Number
Finance	10
Mental health	5
Miscellaneous	5
Part-time work	4
Placement	3
Physical health	3
Home conditions	2
Living conditions	1
Vocational guidance	1
Personality problems	1

The relatively higher frequency of problems of mental health obtained from the records of interviews kept by professors than from the records of students may be explained by the fact that a member of the faculty who is also a psychiatrist is included among the 7 professors who kept records.

2. Problems Regarding Which Personnel Officers Are Consulted

As Reported by Students. Personnel officers are consulted concerning both personal and academic problems, but their counseling function is chiefly with regard to *personal* problems. Nearly two-thirds of the problems reported by students with personnel officers deal with difficulties of this nature. The personal problems on which students most frequently consult personnel officials are part-time work, finance, physical health, living conditions, and placement. Conferences on these 5 types of problems constitute 90 per cent of all conferences with personnel officers on personal problems. How far the type of problem reported by the students was influenced by seasonal factors cannot be determined without further sampling at different times of year, but the time during which the data were gathered seemed to be as free from seasonal peculiarities as any that could be chosen.

Over 90 per cent of the conferences on academic problems pertain to courses, degrees, and study. Nearly all the conferences regarding courses deal with getting desired courses, choice of major, and choice of courses. Forty-two of the 74 conferences on degrees concern requirements for a degree and 13 concern the question of whether to work for a degree. Practically all the conferences regarding study pertain to the library and are with librarians. Only 16 per cent of the total number of conferences reported by students on academic problems are with personnel officials.

As Shown by Personnel Officers' Records of Student Interviews. Table XVIII, indicating the frequency with which various types of problems come to each personnel office, confirms students' reports regarding the important rôle of personnel officials in the

TABLE XVIII

FREQUENCY WITH WHICH VARIOUS TYPES OF STUDENT PROBLEMS
ARE BROUGHT TO PERSONNEL OFFICES*

PROBLEM	PERSONNEL OFFICES									
	Com. on High-er De-grees	Office of Sec-re-tary	Bur. of Educ. Serv.	Bus. Mgr.	Au-ditor	Part-Time	Stud. Org.	Wel-fare Di-rec-tor	Total	Per Cent of Total
Academic	31	129						5	165	18.0
Mental health	1							4	5	0.5
Physical health								69	69	7.5
Leisure, recreation, clubs							5	26	31	3.4
Social relationships							5	17	22	2.4
Living conditions		4		44				10	58	6.3
Finance				10	20			24	54	5.9
Home conditions								5	5	0.5
Religion								1	1	0.1
Part-time work			6	2		146	2	7	163	17.8
Placement, vocational guidance		1	230					2	233	25.5
Time distribution	1							2	3	0.3
Adjustment to physical environment								40	40	4.4
Personality problems ...								9	9	1.0
Miscellaneous		2		8			2	46	58	6.4
Total	33	136	236	64	20	146	14	267	916	100.0
No. of people in office keeping records	1	7	7	4	1	1	3	6		

* Number estimated on two-week basis.

solution of personal problems. Interviews on personal problems constitute 82 per cent of the total number of interview records. The table shows, however, that not all personnel offices are chiefly concerned with personal problems. The Office of the Secretary and the Office of the Committee on Higher Degrees deal almost exclusively with academic problems.

The specialization in the type of problem with which the various offices deal is also clearly shown in Table XVIII. With the exception of the Office of the Welfare Director, which deals with many types of personal problems, each office concentrates on student problems of one or two types. The Office of the Secretary and of the Committee on Higher Degrees specialize, as has been pointed out, in academic problems; the Office of Student Organizations, in problems of recreation and of social relationships; the Office of the Business Manager, in living conditions and finance; the Office of the Auditor, in finance; the Bureau of Educational Service, in problems of vocational placement and vocational guidance; and the Bureau of Part-Time Employment, as the name implies, in problems of part-time positions.

Considering the size of the student body, the number of personal contacts between personnel officers and students seems relatively small. According to statements made by personnel officers, the period during which the records were kept was a comparatively quiet time and does not represent the offices at the peak of their student contacts. The Secretary's Office, the Auditor's Office, and

TABLE XIX

COMPARISON OF FREQUENCY WITH WHICH VARIOUS STUDENT PROBLEMS ARE BROUGHT TO PERSONNEL OFFICERS, AS SHOWN BY STUDENTS' REPORTS AND INTERVIEW RECORDS OF PERSONNEL OFFICERS

PROBLEM	STUDENTS' REPORTS	PERSONNEL OFFICERS' RECORDS
	Per Cent	Per Cent
Academic work	37.0	18.0
Finance	12.7	5.9
Leisure	2.1	3.4
Part-time work	14.5	17.8
Placement	9.3	25.5
Social relationships	1.7	2.4
Living conditions	9.7	6.3
Physical health	10.2	7.5
Time distribution	0.2	0.3
Professional problems	0.8	0.0
Mental health	1.2	0.5
Home conditions	0.2	0.5
Religion	0.0	0.1
Miscellaneous problems	0.0	6.4
Physical environment	0.0	4.4
Personality problems	0.4	1.0

the Business Manager's Office, for example, would show a much larger number of interviews during registration periods. The Bureau of Educational Service makes its largest number of contacts in the spring.

Comparison of Frequency with Which Student Problems Come to Personnel Officers as Shown by Students' Reports and Interview Records. Students report a higher percentage of conferences with personnel officers on academic problems than the interview records show. The percentage of conferences reported by students is increased by the fact that conferences with librarians are included. Students also report a higher percentage of conferences with personnel officers on finance than the interview records indicate. The fact that the Provost's interviews with students with regard to loans are not included in the records of personnel officers accounts in part for the difference. The greatest discrepancy in the two reports is in the percentage of consultations on placement. Students' reports show that 9 per cent of the conferences with personnel officers are regarding placement; interview records indicate that 25 per cent are concerning this question. This difference is due in part to the inclusion in the records of the Bureau of Educational Service of all contacts with students, such as requests for registration blanks, change of student's address, and the like. The students, on the other hand, however, tend to report only those conferences to which they attach considerable significance.

KINDS OF ASSISTANCE GIVEN BY COLLEGE OFFICIALS IN THE SOLUTION OF STUDENT PROBLEMS

After the types of problems which students bring to personnel officers and faculty members have been ascertained, the further question arises as to whether these contacts are helpful to the students. Two bases of judging the helpfulness of the conferences are available—judgments of students and records of the action taken by personnel officers and professors concerning the various types of problems which came to them during the period in which interview records were kept.

1. *Helpfulness of Conferences as Reported by Students*

The percentage of conferences considered helpful on personal and on academic problems is almost the same. Students who report regarding the helpfulness of conferences consider 80 per cent of conferences on personal problems and 82 per cent of conferences on academic problems helpful.   The three personal problems showing the lowest percentage of helpful conferences are placement, part-time work, and living conditions.   In none of these except placement is the percentage below 70.

The work of the Bureau of Educational Service cannot be adequately judged by the percentage of helpful conferences reported on the Student Inquiry Blanks.   In the first place, not all problems are equally easy of solution.   The problem of placement is one of the most difficult of those problems in the solution of which the college endeavors to assist students.

The problem of the student who does not know how to use the library is much more readily soluble than the problem of a student in need of a position.   Furthermore, many students who have obtained desirable positions through the assistance of the Bureau are no longer in school, while those who have failed to obtain positions may tend to continue in school until they do find work.   The reports may be unduly weighted by this factor.

Problems of part-time work are also problems of placement, and their solution presents on a smaller scale the same kinds of difficulties.   Here, as in the matter of placement, personnel officers are restricted, by the number of positions available, in their ability to assist students.

The fact that a low percentage of helpful conferences may be due to factors at the present time outside the ability of the personnel officers to control is shown also in problems of living conditions.   Conferences with personnel officers cannot be of much assistance in solving problems which arise from fundamental lacks in the dormitories themselves.

Specific ways in which students state that conferences have been helpful to them follow.

Personal Problems—

    Finance—

        Made very practical suggestions as to where I might borrow money.

        Conference resulted in a grant through one of the foundations.

        Informed me about Student Bank on the campus.

        Helpful to share problem with someone who seemed interested.

        Arranged with Auditor to pay tuition monthly.

Part-time work—

Helped me find a place where I could work for my room and board.

Helped me secure work in the college cafeteria.

Encouraged me to go ahead with my plan of part-time work which in the end paid nearly all my expenses.

Helped me locate a minor position.

Placement—

Pointed out future possibilities in the field.

Obtained a position close enough to the college to permit me to continue study.

Professor referred me to the Bureau of Educational Service.

Academic Problems—

Requirements for degree—

Permitted me to substitute six points of history for six required points in education.

Helped me arrange a definite program for all requirements that are to be fulfilled for the degree of Master of Science.

Was clear about what I had to do to complete requirements.

Choice of courses and major—

Talked with me to determine what I most needed and most wanted, then advised courses accordingly.

Helped me to evaluate courses in terms of my needs.

Gave résumé of each course and pointed out advantages and disadvantages.

Worked out with me a list of useful courses.

Points that were not clear in my mind were explained.

Placed before me a definite plan for improvement in special skills.

Dissertation—

Helped in suggesting source material.

Suggested research which was needed in my field.

Library—

A week-card was granted for reserve books.

A part-time student's card was given me.

Told me of Orientation Tour which helped me a great deal.

2. Helpfulness of Conferences as Indicated by Interview Records of Personnel Officers and Professors

A better understanding of the ways in which conferences with personnel officers and professors aid in the solution of students' problems may be obtained from the records of action taken by personnel officers in various types of problems.

Action Taken Regarding Financial Problems. The financial problems brought to the Auditor's Office were treated as follows:

Extension of time in the payment of fees granted to the five students who requested it.
Loan to student authorized.
Satisfactory arrangement made with student whose check was returned.

Financial problems which came to the Business Manager's Office were chiefly concerning the place or time of making payments on rent. The information requested was given. One member of the faculty took the following action with regard to financial problems:

Made small personal gift to student.
Referred student who needed a loan to the Provost.
Wrote letters introducing foreign students to officers in foundations.

Action Taken Regarding Placement Problems. The following types of action were taken by the Bureau of Educational Service in 236 interviews concerning student problems:

	Number	Per Cent
Discussed situation	65	25
No action required	42	16
Referred student to:		
Member of faculty	12	5
Part-time office	11	4
Other person in bureau	13	5
Outside agency or organization	4	1
Gave information	28	11
Arranged for interview	26	10
Checked files or filled blanks	16	6
Suggested other position to follow up	7	3
Sent credentials	3	1
Action not specified	35	13

In the opinion of the Bureau, the time of year accounts for the large proportion of merely preparatory interviews. All the steps recorded—filing credentials, discussion of possibilities in a specific field, and best academic preparation; inquiry concerning positions, notification of a possible position, arranging for interview with employer, and reporting on interview with employer and action taken—seem to be essential to the process of securing a position. Records kept later in the year would probably show a larger proportion of interviews leading more directly to the securing of positions.

Action Taken Regarding Problems of Part-Time Work. Fourteen, or 19 per cent, of the 73 students who were interviewed by the staff of the Bureau of Part-Time Employment during the period in which the interview records were kept were placed as a result of the interview. Only 5 of these students were placed in positions for which they had expressed preference. In 68 per cent of the interviews the solution of the problem was pending. Five per cent of the students were referred to other agencies.

The types of action taken by the Bureau were as follows:

Filed student's request for work.
Asked student to call again. No suitable position at present available.
Told student to keep up courage.
Talked with student about possibilities other than the special type of work desired.
Tested applicant's ability to do the work desired.
Told student about a possible position.
Gave names and addresses of firms or persons from whom position might be secured.
Arranged for appointment with employer.
Sent student out on a job.
Sent student out on a temporary job and asked him to return to make arrangements concerning another position.
Referred student to member of Bureau of Educational Service staff for permanent work.

Types of problems for which no solution was found were those in which there was no position available, those in which the student was not qualified for the positions available, and one in which the position for which the student had been recommended had already been filled. The student had delayed in making application.

Action Taken Regarding Academic Problems. The assistance given with regard to various types of academic problems may be seen from the following examples of action taken by the staff of the Secretary's Office with regard to problems of this nature:

Gave the information desired—
Concerning requirements for degrees.
Concerning credit given in late registration.
Concerning licenses to teach in New York state.
Concerning transcript of record.

Referred student to someone else for information—
To professors:
for more detailed information concerning courses.
for permission to carry given program.
To another member of Secretary's office:
for specialized information.
To another official of the college:
for approval of program.
for specialized information.
To another college in the university:
for information about their requirements.
To principal of high school:
for special information.

Secured copies of transcripts for students.
Evaluated previous work.
Sent for additional records.
Made adjustment of requirements—

Reduced requirements.
Granted exemptions.
Granted exemptions on satisfactory completion of work.
Granted extension of time.
Removed deficiency on basis of reconsideration of student's record.

Helped student plan program—
Adjusted conflicts in program.
Planned program for several terms ahead.
Made adjustments in records needed in changing major.

PROBLEMS WHICH STUDENTS ATTEMPT TO SOLVE WITHOUT ASSIST-
ANCE OF PERSONNEL OFFICERS AND PROFESSORS

Academic Problems. It appears that many kinds of personal and academic problems are not being brought either to personnel officers or to professors. Of the 74 kinds of academic problems reported by students, 21 were brought to personnel officers and 19 to professors during the period in which the interview records were kept. Six kinds of problems were brought to both personnel officers and professors, leaving 40 kinds of problems reported by students which did not come to the attention of either personnel officers or professors.

Kinds of problems which appear in personnel officers' records more than twice are:

	Number
Satisfying entrance requirements	40
Registration	15
Requirements for degree	13
Evaluation of credits	11
Reduction of requirements	10
Preparation for matriculation	8
Dissertation	7
Request for extension of time in which to complete requirements	6
Choice of courses	5
Choice of major	4
Sponsor for dissertation	4

These interview records indicate that the preponderance of academic problems which come to personnel officers appears to be of a technical and somewhat routine nature. The fact that nearly half of the interviews are less than ten minutes in length seems to substantiate this statement. Academic problems brought to professors show a smaller proportion of problems of this type.

Many of the more complex problems reported by students do not appear in the records of either the personnel officers or the professors. The following are examples of these kinds of problems:

> Difficulty with courses
> How heavy a schedule to carry
> Lack of systematic study habits
> Maintaining a satisfactory academic standing
> Degree of specialization within the major field
> Conflict between remunerative work and classes
> Covering required work

Personal Problems. Problems of mental health are brought infrequently to both personnel officers and professors. Professors' interview records indicate that one professor only was consulted regarding problems of this type. This concentration is probably desirable, since such problems require in many cases expert assistance. Some of the problems mentioned by students, such as "unable to sleep at night because of worry over academic work," "worried about completing my work," might be alleviated by consultation with the professor directly concerned.

Problems of leisure and recreation are reported frequently by students, but college officials are seldom consulted concerning them. The Social Directors in the residence halls for women make useful and practical contacts in arranging for the sale of theater and concert tickets and assisting students in keeping in touch with the recreational facilities offered in the city. The major kinds of student problems which concern lack of time and opportunity for leisure are not included in personnel officers' records.

Students do not consult college officials frequently with regard to problems of social relationships. The contacts of the Office of Student Organizations are largely of an administrative rather than a personal nature. The majority of consultations on problems of this type are with the staff of the Office of Welfare Director.

Problems of personality, home conditions, religion, adjustment to the physical environment, and time distribution are rarely brought to college officials for consultation.

DEGREE TO WHICH STUDENTS' PROBLEMS ARE BEING SOLVED

Personal Problems. As Table XX indicates, students have solved satisfactorily one-fourth of their personal problems, have found a partial solution to slightly over one-fifth, have been un-

TABLE XX

DEGREE TO WHICH PERSONAL PROBLEMS REPORTED BY 1,000 STUDENTS HAVE BEEN SOLVED

PROBLEM	DEGREE OF SOLUTION							
	Not Indicated		Unsolved		Partial		Satisfactory	
	No.	%	No.	%	No.	%	No.	%
Finance	29	13.1	53	24.0	34	15.4	105	47.5
Leisure	36	23.2	62	40.0	57	36.8	0	0.0
Part-time work	22	14.5	51	33.6	12	7.9	67	44.0
Placement	40	26.6	86	57.4	10	6.7	14	9.3
Social relationship	34	25.7	52	39.4	46	34.9	0	0.0
Living conditions	17	15.7	30	27.8	11	10.2	50	46.3
Physical health	9	9.8	12	13.0	29	31.5	42	45.7
Time distribution	19	25.4	15	20.0	30	39.9	11	14.7
Professional problems	7	14.3	18	36.7	0	0.0	24	49.0
Mental health	14	28.6	14	28.6	17	34.7	4	8.2
Home conditions	6	22.2	8	29.6	10	37.1	3	11.1
Religion	1	5.5	6	39.0	11	55.5	0	0.0
Miscellaneous	5	29.4	6	35.3	2	11.8	4	23.5
Physical environment	5	35.7	3	21.4	6	42.9	0	0.0
Personality problems	6	42.9	6	42.9	2	14.2	0	0.0
Total	250	19.6	422	33.1	277	21.8	324	25.5

able to solve one-third, and indicate no solution to one-fifth of their personal problems.

Professional problems have the highest percentage of satisfactory solutions. Nearly one-half of these problems have been solved in a satisfactory manner. Other problems which show a high percentage of satisfactory solutions are finance, part-time work, living conditions, and physical health. It is of interest to note that all these problems also have a high percentage of consultations with college officials.

Academic Problems. As is shown in Table XXI, students' reports indicate that they have been able to solve satisfactorily a somewhat higher percentage of their academic problems than of their personal problems. Thirty-three per cent of academic problems have been solved satisfactorily, 15 per cent have been par-

TABLE XXI

DEGREE TO WHICH ACADEMIC PROBLEMS REPORTED BY 1,000 STUDENTS
HAVE BEEN SOLVED

PROBLEMS PERTAINING TO	SOLUTION									
	Not In-dicated		Unsolved		Unsatis-factory		Partial		Satis-factory	
	No.	%	No.	%	No.	%	No.	%	No.	%
Courses	117	18.4	103	16.1	54	8.4	108	16.9	257	40.2
Degrees and certificates	66	18.5	107	30.0	16	4.5	30	8.4	138	38.6
Study	58	30.9	47	25.0	43	22.9	14	7.4	26	13.8
General advisement	23	23.0	24	24.0	9	9.0	16	16.0	28	28.0
Personal and professional de-velopment	12	16.2	15	20.3	5	6.8	11	14.9	31	41.8
Academic standing	15	23.1	22	33.8	5	7.7	15	23.1	8	12.3
Lacks in physical environment	4	10.2	15	38.5	2	5.1	16	41.1	2	5.1
Lacks in student's training ..	4	13.8	5	17.2	2	6.9	14	48.3	4	13.8
Miscellaneous	8	30.8	6	23.1	4	15.4	3	11.5	5	19.2
Total	307	20.3	344	22.6	140	9.2	227	15.0	499	32.9

tially solved, 23 per cent remain unsolved, 9 per cent have been solved in a manner unsatisfactory to the student, and for 20 per cent of the problems no solution is indicated.

Problems pertaining to personal and professional development, courses, and degrees and certificates show a fairly high percentage of satisfactory solutions. All these problems are frequently brought to college officers for conference.

SUMMARY

A study of the processes by which students solve their problems, as shown by their own reports and by interview records kept by personnel officers and professors during a limited period of time, indicates:

1. Students more frequently consult college officials regarding academic than regarding personal problems.

2. Members of the faculty are consulted concerning both personal and academic problems, but their chief counseling function is in regard to academic problems.

3. The major counseling function of the personnel offices, with two exceptions, is with regard to personal problems. The two exceptions are the Office of the Secretary and the Office of the Committee on Higher Degrees, which specialize in academic problems.

4. The following types of academic problems are frequently brought for consultation: difficulties pertaining to courses, degrees, and general problems of advisement.

5. Less than one-half of the kinds of academic problems reported by students came to the attention of professors and personnel officials during the period in which interview records were kept.

6. Academic problems which require technical information to aid in their solution frequently come to personnel officers. Problems of more complex types appear less frequently in the interview records.

7. The personal problems regarding which students frequently consult college officials are: part-time work, physical health, living conditions, placement, professional problems, and finance.

8. Students seldom confer with college officers concerning personal problems of the following types: religion, time distribution, adjustment to the physical environment, leisure, and social relationships.

9. Each personnel office specializes in some type of problem, with the exception of the Office of the Welfare Director, to which many types of both personal and academic problems come.

10. Students who report concerning the helpfulness of conferences with college officials regard 81 per cent of the conferences as helpful in the solution of their problems.

11. Students have solved satisfactorily one-third of their academic problems and one-fourth of their personal problems.

12. With the exception of problems of placement, personal and academic problems which are frequently brought to college officers show a higher percentage of satisfactory solutions than those which are rarely brought for conference.

Chapter XIV

SUMMARY

THE first chapter stated that the present study would endeavor to answer six definite questions regarding the problems of students in an urban graduate school of education. The information available to answer these six questions is presented in this summary.

1. *What Do the Students Themselves Report as Their Major Personal and Academic Problems during Their Period of Study in the Institution?* Judged by the frequency with which they are mentioned, the major personal problems of students are finance, leisure and recreation, part-time work, placement, and social relationships. By the same criterion, the most important academic problems pertain to courses, degrees and certificates, study, and general advisement. The following eleven problems constitute 79 per cent of all academic problems reported: getting desired courses, choice of courses, use of the library, requirements for a degree, choice of a major, whether to work for a degree, advisement, academic standing, covering required work, dissertation and research, and how heavy a schedule to carry.

2. *Are Certain Problems Characteristic of Special Groups?* Problems of finance rank first in frequency for the entire group and are prevalent in all groups. Men report financial problems more frequently than women. Full-time men students report them more often than the part-time men group.

Problems of leisure and recreation are especially characteristic of full-time students, ranking second in the entire group of full-time students, first with the full-time women group, and first with the full-time "unsigned" group.

Problems of part-time work are mentioned most frequently by the youngest students and by the new students.

Placement is reported as a major problem more often by the youngest and oldest age groups, and by men.

Problems of social relationships rank first with part-time

women students. There is a decided contrast in the frequency with which problems of this nature are reported by the married and unmarried students. Five per cent of married students and 16 per cent of single students report problems in this area.

Difficulties in regard to living conditions and time distribution are more characteristic of full-time women than of other groups.

Physical health is mentioned most frequently as a problem by the anonymous group, particularly by full-time students in this division. It is reported with increasing frequency from the youngest to the oldest age group.

Professional problems are reported by a higher percentage of anonymous part-time students than by any other group.

3. *Which Problems Are Students Bringing for Conference to Officers of the College? Which Officers Are Being Consulted Most Frequently on the Various Kinds of Problems?* Students are more inclined to consult college officials regarding academic problems than regarding personal problems. Of the personal problems a relatively high percentage of problems of part-time work, physical health, living conditions, placement, and professional problems are brought for consultation to officers of the college. The three personal problems highest in actual number of consultations are finance, part-time work, and placement. The percentage of problems of religion, adjustment to the physical environment, time distribution, leisure, and social relationships concerning which college officers are consulted is small. Students frequently consult college officials concerning the following academic problems: courses, degrees, and general problems of academic advisement.

Members of the faculty are consulted frequently concerning both personal and academic problems, but their major counseling function is in regard to academic problems. Eighty-four per cent of all conferences reported by students on academic problems are with professors.

Personnel officers are also consulted with regard to both personal and academic problems, but chiefly concerning personal problems. Two personnel offices, however, deal largely with academic problems.

While professors are consulted concerning a wide variety of problems, personnel officers tend to specialize in certain problems. Academic problems come to the Office of the Secretary and to the

Committee on Higher Degrees; financial problems, to the Office of the Business Manager and of the Auditor; living conditions, to the Office of the Business Manager; problems of part-time work, to the Bureau of Part-Time Employment; and problems of placement, to the Bureau of Educational Service. The Office of the Welfare Director is the only personnel office which is not highly specialized as to the type of problems handled. This office deals with a variety of problems.

4. *Do the Students Regard These Conferences as Helpful?* Students who reported regarding the helpfulness of conferences with college officials consider 80 per cent of conferences on personal problems and 82 per cent of conferences on academic problems helpful in the solution of their difficulties. In the group of personal problems, placement shows the lowest percentage of helpful conferences; in the group of academic problems study shows the lowest percentage.

5. *How Are the Problems Being Solved?* The group of students interviewed are solving their personal problems in a variety of ways. The largest number of those having financial problems are borrowing from friends and relatives. The amount most frequently borrowed is in the $500 to $999 interval.

The problem of part-time work most frequently cited is obtaining part-time work. Less than half of the students citing this problem have found a satisfactory solution to it. The part-time positions most frequently held by students who reported are teaching positions and assistantships.

The placement problem most frequently reported is that of obtaining a position at the close of the academic year. It is too early in the year for most problems of this type to have been solved.

Few students have been able to solve their problems of leisure and recreation. The most frequently occurring problem for which they have found no solution is lack of time for leisure.

Problems of social relationships arise largely from lack of social contacts due most frequently to lack of time and lack of opportunity to make social contacts. Problems in this area are not being satisfactorily solved to any large degree.

Solutions to academic problems are so specific that general statements regarding the manner of solving problems of this nature can hardly be made. The entire group of academic problems shows a somewhat higher percentage of satisfactory solutions than the personal problems.

6. *What Student Problems Are Not Being Adequately Solved at Present?* Problems of finance, part-time work, living conditions, physical health, and professional matters are being satisfactorily solved by 40 to 50 per cent of the students reporting them.

Satisfactory solutions of problems of leisure, social relationships, and placement are reported by a minority of students. The majority of the personal problems infrequently mentioned are not being solved adequately.

Of the six types of academic problems most frequently reported, problems of study, academic standing, and general advisement are being satisfactorily solved by the smallest percentage of students.

In brief, the study shows that the graduate students studied, as well as the undergraduates, have a wide range of unsolved problems both personal and academic, that they consult college officials with regard to all types of problems, and that they find over three-fourths of their conferences helpful in the solution of their problems.

Chapter XV

IMPLICATIONS OF THE PRESENT STUDY TO THE FURTHER DEVELOPMENT OF THE PERSONNEL PROGRAM IN A GRADUATE SCHOOL OF EDUCATION

The chief value of the present inquiry lies in the contribution it may make to the better understanding of the problems of graduate students. A knowledge of the problems of the group of which the student is a member may suggest to instructors and personnel officers a starting point for ascertaining the special problems of any one student.

There are, however, certain implications to be drawn from the findings of the present study which may be of assistance in planning the future personnel program of the college. A personnel program exists for the benefit of the students whom it serves. A knowledge of the problems of students and of the additional services desired by students offers one basis on which the present personnel program of an institution may be developed and expanded.

As was pointed out in the first chapter, this inquiry is only one phase of the investigation being made by a graduate school of education to ascertain the effectiveness of its present program and to determine the modifications needed. The suggestions made in this chapter are based primarily upon the findings of the present study with regard to the problems of students. They will no doubt be modified when the findings of the entire body of facts from all phases of the study are assembled and analyzed.

The chief value of this investigation to other graduate schools of education probably lies in its description of a method of investigation which appears to be of value in revealing problems of students and in suggesting areas in which the present personnel program may be improved rather than in a direct application of the findings to institutions dissimilar in certain respects.

The Need of Personnel Services. Kelly characterizes the graduate schools as "centers of intellectual life where each graduate student is pursuing his own line of research and where the emphasis is not upon the development of the student, but upon the expansion of the bounds of human knowledge."[1] The *Seventh Yearbook of the Department of Superintendence* states that the graduate school has two aims:

1. To teach properly prepared students the most advanced and specialized phases of the subjects offered by the university, and

2. To increase the sum total of human knowledge through research.[2]

Both these statements seem to give a rather narrow conception of the function of the graduate school of education. The majority of the students plan to enter some phase of educational work. Since one important element in their professional success, as well as in their personal happiness, will be their satisfactory adjustment in many life situations, it appears that one important function of a graduate school of education should be not only to promote research and stimulate the student intellectually but to contribute to the development of the entire personality of the student.

The findings of the present study show definitely the need of personnel services in the graduate school of education under consideration. Problems reported by students cover many areas. They are of a serious nature, involving questions such as the professional future, scholastic success, and physical and mental health of students.

The need of personnel services, however, is shown not so much by the mere existence of problems as by the inability of the students to solve them without assistance. Perhaps graduate students should be able to solve their own problems satisfactorily without assistance, but as a matter of fact the majority of students in the present study are not doing so. Only one-third of the academic problems and one-fourth of the personal problems reported by students have been satisfactorily solved. College officials were consulted concerning nearly one-half of the problems reported by students. The results of this investigation do not substantiate the assumption that graduate students can solve their problems alone.

[1] R. L. Kelly, *Tendencies in College Administration*, p. 99. Lancaster, Pa.: The Science Press, 1925.

[2] Department of Superintendence, *Seventh Yearbook*, p. 311. Washington, D. C.: National Education Association, 1929.

Extent to Which the Present Personnel Program Is Meeting Student Needs. There are the following evidences that the present personnel program is meeting student needs to some extent:

1. A number of students report no problems.
2. Many students mention the assistance they have received from officials of the college in the solution of their problems.

The fact that 135 of the 1,000 students who returned the Student Inquiry Blanks cited no problems of any kind indicates that these students either are solving their own problems without assistance or have found the services offered at present adequate. Members of this group, as well as a number of the students who reported problems which had been solved, stated voluntarily, "I have found the personnel services entirely satisfactory."

Another indication that students consider the personnel work of value is the fact that they report 80 per cent of their conferences with college officials helpful. A much larger percentage of helpful conferences than of satisfactory solutions are reported on many of these problems—a fact which seems to suggest that students recognize that personnel officers may be doing everything in their power to assist them in solving their problems but that there are often conditions beyond the control of the college officials which prevent the problem from being brought to a satisfactory solution. For example, the amount of the loan fund and the scholarship fund limits the extent to which the college can assist students financially; the number of available positions circumscribes the work of the Bureaus of Educational Service and of Part-time Employment. It suggests also that students consider conferences helpful if they make even a preparatory step toward the solution of a problem. Some conferences were reported helpful in which the counselor simply "offered encouragement," "told me to keep up courage," or "seemed interested in my problem."

Further evidence of the effectiveness of the personnel work is that, on the whole, problems about which college officials are frequently consulted show a higher percentage of satisfactory solutions than problems about which they are rarely consulted. Problems of placement illustrate the variation between the percentage of conferences regarded as helpful and the percentage which are brought to a successful conclusion. Although a small percentage of satisfactory outcomes of interviews of this type is reported, owing in part probably to the time of year at which the reports were made, over two-thirds of the conferences are considered helpful. Students distinguish between the conferences in which an effort is made to help them and those in which the counselor makes no real attempt to give assistance.

The present organization appears to deal most effectively with problems which are of a definite nature, such as meeting requirements for a degree, meeting requirements for entrance to the college, and locating a lawyer, dentist, or doctor for professional services. Many of the failures of students to solve problems of this type have been due to their lack of knowledge about whom to consult rather than to inadequate provision for counseling. The absence of problems pertaining to the routine of registration also suggests the effectiveness with which the administrative details of dealing with student problems are handled.

The present organization appears to deal rather less effectively with such problems as finance, part-time work, living conditions, and physical health. Personnel officers are frequently consulted about problems of this kind and satisfactory solutions are reported in about half of the cases. Judged by the number of conferences on placement problems which were considered helpful, these problems should be included in this group.

The problems which appear to be least effectively dealt with are:

1. The social and recreational needs of students.

2. Complex types of problems such as problems of mental hygiene, personality, home conditions, religion, and adjustment to physical environment.

3. The difficult and complicated problems of academic advisement.

Reports of students and records of personnel officers show that college officials are rarely consulted concerning problems of these kinds. Few of these problems are being satisfactorily solved at present. The low percentage of satisfactory solutions appears to be due both to the fact that many of the problems are difficult to solve and to the fact that provision for their solution is at present inadequate.

Suggestions for Additional Services. Certain assumptions regarding the nature of a personnel program underlie the following suggestions for additional personnel services:

1. One of the important functions of a graduate school of education is the development of the individual student.

2. Future developments in personnel work should be based upon the present program, which has evolved in response to definite needs in the institution.

3. One of the major functions of personnel work should be to prevent problems of a nonconstructive kind from arising.

4. Trained personnel workers should be in command of techniques for solving problems and of sources of information regarding problem solution which may not be known to the student.

5. Important problems of students cannot be dealt with in a meager amount of time. Technical questions dealing with ascertaining requirements for a degree, or sources of medical service may be dealt with briefly. Problems such as choice of major, decision as to whether to continue graduate study, and worry over academic work require that the counselor have ample time for a thorough consideration of the many factors involved in the situation.

The college makes some provision at present for meeting the social and recreational needs of students. The social functions of the Graduate Club, the departmental clubs, the educational fraternities, and the dormitories are all the result of efforts to provide a social program for students.

There appear to be two factors involved in developing a program which will meet the social demands of graduate students more effectively than the present one. The first is that the social program should be under the supervision of someone skilled in ascertaining and in providing the kinds of social functions which are satisfying to students and which contribute to their social development. The second is that students must allow time in their schedules for activities of a social nature. In the interviews, students expressed little desire for formal social affairs, but frequently requested small gatherings in which professors and students could meet informally. Many students expressed the desire to have more contacts with professors outside the classroom.

Planning a recreational program will also involve more than providing additional physical facilities. The most noticeable weakness of the recreational programs of students, as stated in the interviews and as shown in the time schedules, is the lack of physical exercise. Students recognize the desirability of planning for some systematic physical recreation, but because facilities are not readily available and because the students do not provide a definite time in their schedules for it, they fail to secure it.

With the restricted amount of leisure time which students have, they must be able to get their physical recreation with as little preparatory effort as possible. One of the difficulties which students find now in securing physical exercise is that the facilities of the college are not available at the times when they are free to use them.

Students suggested in the interviews that the college could render a distinct service by providing facilities for physical recreation in each housing unit. They asked in particular that space and equipment for deck tennis, handball, and volley ball be provided on the roofs of the college apartment houses which are adapted to such uses. Simple facilities for recreation in these smaller units might be more widely used than equipment provided in one central place, such as the gymnasium.

The social and recreational problems of students are closely related. Students find social companionship in recreation and find relaxation and recreation in certain types of social functions. A well-planned program of one type will aid in the solution of problems of the other type.

The need of counsel on the more complex personal problems of students was clearly evident in the interviews. Although the interviewers had no official connection with the college and were in no position to offer assistance to students, a number of students came to the interviews with the hope of obtaining assistance in solving some of their perplexing problems. The interviewers were repeatedly asked to suggest someone to whom the student might go for assistance. It was not uncommon for a student to ask "What would you suggest that I do about this problem?"

The question may be raised whether it is the function of the college to assist students in the solution of problems such as those involving religion, home conditions, and emotional adjustments. The seriousness of problems of these types in the group interviewed leads the writer to believe that the college would render a real service to students if it could genuinely help them with their complicated personal problems. In some cases these problems are interfering seriously with the academic work of the student and with his professional success.

The fact that problems of this kind are decidedly delicate to handle indicates that if any attempt is made to meet them the assistance offered must be expert. Two types of assistance seem to be called for. The first is a wise counselor to whom a student could go to discuss his problems. This person should be one for whose character and academic achievements students have respect and admiration. Many students are probably receiving this kind of counsel at present from a professor or other member of the college staff whom they know. Some students, however, are not receiving assistance and do not know to whom to turn for it. The second kind of assistance needed is that of counselors technically trained along special lines. The general counselor should be able to refer students who need expert assistance to the proper sources. The college offers courses in mental hygiene, and two professors devote time to assisting students in the solution of problems of this nature. There is, however, no one whose major function is to deal with the problems of mental hygiene.

Problems of mental health are probably more prevalent than the present inquiry reveals. The fact that the questionnaire, which is decidedly not adapted to the discovery of problems of this nature, disclosed some problems of this kind suggests that refined methods would find the problems more widespread. Hopkins[3] found that nine of the fourteen institutions which he studied were making definite provision for mental hygiene services. The tendency was to relate the work definitely to the health program and to tie it closely to the work of the medical staff, as well as to the work of the psychologists. An extension of the services being offered at present and the official recognition of the work as part of the health program of the college seem desirable.

The interviews with students show clearly that they feel the need of more careful advisement on difficult academic problems than they are receiving at present. In the opinion of the writer, the desire of students for better academic advisement was the most important finding of the interviews, as they relate to the personnel program.

The professors carry the burden of academic counseling at present. The three most common difficulties which they encounter in advising students under the present system are: lack of information about the student, lack of knowledge regarding vocational

[3] *Op. cit.*, p. 7.

opportunities in different fields, and lack of time to advise the student adequately. The adviser is handicapped by knowing little about the student who comes to him for counsel during registration. In the majority of cases, the student is a stranger to him. No application blanks, no test results, no information from previous interviews are available to the person whose duty it is to assist students in selecting the courses which will be most useful to them.

The adviser's lack of knowledge of the vocational opportunities in different fields is an especially serious handicap to his giving adequate guidance to students who are trying to choose a major field in which to specialize. In some fields, facts are available concerning the number of positions in the field, the turnover among the occupants of the present positions and the possibilities of new positions being created. This knowledge, however, is usually possessed only by professors in the major field concerned. They do not know about the vocational openings in other fields.

The lack of time to give to each individual student during registration makes it impossible to supplement adequately the advisers' limited knowledge of the student.

Four common difficulties which face the student who is choosing his program are the great number of courses from which he must choose, uncertainty as to the content of the courses, uncertainty as to the field in which he wishes to specialize, and conflicts between the courses he wants to take and those which he is required to take in order to obtain a degree.

The new student in particular is in need of careful counsel regarding his program. He is confronted with approximately 800 courses from which he is expected to choose those which best fit his needs. His knowledge of the content of the courses is probably limited to the catalogue descriptions. If he knows the field in which he wishes to work and has definitely decided upon his major, his path is comparatively easy. If, however, he does not "fit in" with this system and is uncertain concerning his choice of major, he finds difficulty in obtaining counsel. There are advisers to suggest courses within a given field but not to help him in his most important decision, that of choosing the field to which he is to devote the major portion of his time.

The fourth difficulty, that of conflict between the courses desired and those required for a degree, is only in part a matter of advisement; it is more a matter of the policy of the college. The adviser's function here may be to show the student the reasonableness of the requirements.

These difficulties of advisement might be somewhat alleviated in the following ways: (1) by making available to the adviser information about the students who will probably come to him for advice; (2) by appointing certain advisers whose special function is to consult with students who are undecided in their choice of major; (3) by providing more time per student for conference with his adviser either at registration or during the ten days following registration in which the student is at liberty to change his program.

It might be possible to obtain from the prospective student, as part of the routine of application for admission, significant information concerning his previous training and present interests and abilities which could be given, prior to registration, to a professor in the candidate's chosen major field. Likewise the data concerning candidates who have not selected their major subjects could be passed on to the special advisers of this group of students.

One of the special functions of the advisers of students who have not chosen their major could be to make available information regarding the opportunities in various fields. In cases in which the adviser did not have the information at hand to answer students' questions, he could refer the student to advisers in special fields.

The fact that information with which to answer students' questions is not at present available indicates the need of research. Researches of the type made by Hager[4] are needed to give a body of information which personnel officers and professors may use as a basis for advising students. Since problems of finance and part-time work are widespread in the student body, both these areas should be studied. Information is needed on such questions as the conditions under which it is wise for students to borrow money for graduate study and as to the advisability of students' attempting to do part-time work while carrying a full-time academic schedule.

The group of people constituting the present personnel staff are largely specialists in some particular phase of the work. Not

[4] *Op. cit.*

only do the personnel offices concentrate on certain types of problems, but the members of the staff within certain offices specialize in some aspect of the problems which come to the attention of that office. This method seems to result in an efficient organization of the work in each separate division. It appears, however, that some plan is needed to coordinate the work now being done in order to prevent waste of students' time in being passed from one person to another, to prevent duplication in services offered, and to provide additional services as the need becomes apparent. One step toward achieving this unification would be to employ a Director of Personnel whose primary interest would be not in the work of a particular office, but in that of the organization as a whole and who could study the entire personnel program from the standpoint of whether it was functioning most effectively for the individual student.

The suggestions which have been made for additional personnel services are in brief:

1. That a more adequate social and recreational program be provided under the direction of persons skilled in ascertaining and providing the kinds of activities which will be satisfying to graduate students.

2. That expert assistance be given students in the solution of their complex personal problems by providing a general counselor and specialists to whom difficult cases may be referred.

3. That more attention be given to counseling students on their important and difficult academic problems. It is suggested that advisers be given more information concerning the students whom they are to guide, more time for their conferences, and a reliable body of material with which to answer students' questions; that special advisers be appointed for those students who are uncertain concerning their choice of major and who want information regarding vocational openings in various fields and regarding the qualifications required to fill those positions.

4. That provision be made for research on personnel problems in order to provide a basis for counseling students more adequately.

5. That coordination of the present work is needed and might be effected through the appointment of a Director of Personnel who would have supervision of the entire personnel program.

These suggestions are made primarily on the basis of the deficiencies in the present program which appear to the writer to be indicated by the reports of students concerning their problems. They represent, therefore, only the students' point of view concerning the personnel services needed and should be so interpreted. They are based also on the composition of the present student body. It is beyond the scope of this study to consider in detail the admissions policy of the college. It is the opinion of the writer that a graduate school of education is entitled to make a careful selection of the students to whom it grants admission. The writer believes, however, that after the college has admitted the student the responsibility devolves upon the college to assist the student to make progress in his work and to aid him in overcoming those factors in his personality or environment which hinder his development. If this point of view be held by the college, it is evident that a careful selection of applicants is desirable.

DESIRABLE FEATURES OF A GUIDANCE PROGRAM IN A GRADUATE SCHOOL OF EDUCATION

Two questions were raised in the first chapter regarding personnel work in a graduate school of education. One question, that of whether graduate students need personnel services, has been considered in the preceding section. The other question, that of whether the same kinds of services should be offered graduates as are offered undergraduates, will be discussed in the present section.

One's first impression in considering the likenesses and differences between the personnel services needed by graduate and undergraduate students is that since the former are a more mature group they will require different types of services. However, when one examines Hopkins'[5] list of the services offered to undergraduates and compares it with the services which graduate students need, as shown by the problems reported by them, one is impressed with the fact that graduates need many of the same types of services as undergraduates. For example, graduates in common with undergraduates have problems of orientation, health, mental hygiene, and employment and placement. It does not appear that there is any one sphere in which graduate students

[5] *Op. cit.*, p. 7.

have solved their problems and in which they no longer need assistance.

The differences in the services needed by the two groups are found in the nature of the specific problems of different types rather than in the general areas of problems. For example, the assumption might be made that students in a graduate school of education have decided upon their vocation and do not need advice on this question. Statements of students show, however, that some are uncertain as to whether they wish to continue in education as a profession, others are uncertain about the field in which they wish to specialize, and a third group are uncertain concerning the best way in which to achieve their vocational objectives. In other words, the advice needed by these graduate students does not cover so wide a range of vocations as that needed by undergraduates, but involves the need of specialized, accurate information regarding various types of positions within the field of education.

Problems in a graduate school of education have an evolutionary aspect. From a positive standpoint there should be a progression from one educational level to another in social and emotional development as well as in academic achievement. This evolutionary aspect of problems may be illustrated in the field of student activities. The graduate student has lost a good deal of his enthusiasm for the undergraduate type of extracurricular activities, but he still needs certain organizations which will contribute to his social development. He feels the futility of participating in activities which contribute little to his growth, but he may welcome activities which aid his social adjustment on a slightly higher level.

There appear to the writer to be two important features which should characterize personnel work in a graduate school of education. The first is that the services should be of an expert character and the second, that the personnel work should have a professional as well as a personal aspect.

The statement that personnel services in a graduate school of education should be expert in character is based on three factors: the complexity of the problems, the relatively short period of residence in the institution, and the experience which the student brings to the solution of his problems.

Many of the serious personal problems of the group of students interviewed were apparently of long standing. A student who has reached the graduate school without having effected a solution to serious problems of personality or of mental hygiene is, by virtue of the fact that his habits are more fixed than those of younger students, a more difficult person to assist in achieving a satisfactory adjustment.

The choice of courses and of major is extremely important to the student who has only one year in which to do his graduate work. He is at a point in his professional career in which a mistake may have far-reaching consequences. His future placement depends in part on the choice of his field of graduate study. The adviser who undertakes to help the student make his choice of courses assumes, whether he is willing or not, a heavy responsibility.

Moreover, graduate students have a considerable background of training and experience. They seek counsel only from those persons whom they believe to be wiser and more experienced than themselves. A counselor must have a wide range of knowledge and experience to advise graduate students effectively.

The second point, that personnel work in a graduate school of education should have a professional as well as a personal aspect, seems especially worthy of emphasis. From the elementary school through the college, teachers are being called upon to do an increasing amount of guidance. The home-room programs of many junior and senior high schools require that the teacher be competent to counsel pupils not only with regard to their choice of subjects, but with regard to more personal problems. A frequent complaint of administrators in secondary schools is that teachers are not equipped to carry out their part of the guidance program.

On the college level instructors are being called upon to counsel students both with regard to their academic plans and with regard to other areas of adjustment. The recent developments at the University of Chicago and at Harvard University illustrate the responsibility that is being placed upon the instructors for the guidance of their students.

If the personnel program of the graduate school of education is well planned, if it contributes to the needs of the individual student in an effective way, it not only will benefit the student by assisting him in the solution of his own immediate problems, but will give him some insight into the counseling process. A student who participates in an interview which advances his own problem toward a solution has the opportunity to observe methods of interviewing, of diagnosing difficulty, and of working out a plan for the solution of the problem which should be of service to him in his later efforts to counsel his own pupils.

In view of these considerations it appears that the graduate school of education has both a unique opportunity and a special responsibility for developing an effective personnel program.

Bibliography

ANGELL, ROBERT COOLEY. *A Study in Undergraduate Adjustment.* Chicago: University of Chicago Press, 1930. Pp. ix + 164.

BINGHAM, WALTER V. AND MOORE, BRUCE V. *How to Interview.* New York: Harper & Brothers, 1931. Pp. 320.

BORAAS, JULIUS. "Troubles of College Freshmen." *School and Society,* VI, 491-494 (October, 1917).

BRAGDON, HELEN D. *Counseling the College Student.* Cambridge: Harvard University Press, 1929. Pp. xi + 162.

CLOTHIER, R. C. "College Principles and Functions." *The Personnel Journal,* X, 9-17 (June, 1931).

COLUMBIA UNIVERSTY ANNUAL REPORTS. *Report of the Dean of Columbia College, 1927.* New York, 1928. Pp. 43-70.

COWLEY, W. H. "A Technique for Making a Student Personnel Survey." *The Personnel Journal,* X, 17-26 (June, 1931).

DEPARTMENT OF SUPERINTENDENCE. *Seventh Yearbook.* Washington, D. C.: Department of Superintendence, 1929. Pp. 616.

EDWARDS, R. H. *Factors in Student Counseling.* Mimeographed copy, 1929. Pp. 133.

GATES, ARTHUR I. *Psychology for Students of Education.* New York: The Macmillan Company, 1931. Pp. xv + 612.

GREEN, GERALDINE. "Freshman Problems." *Proceedings of the National Association of Deans of Women,* Washington, D. C., Association, 1929. Pp. 152-154.

GREY, EDWARD, FIRST VISCOUNT OF FALLODON. *Recreation.* Boston: Houghton Mifflin Company, 1920. Pp. ii + 42.

HAGER, WALTER E. *The Quest for Vocational Adjustment in the Profession of Education.* New York: Bureau of Publications, Teachers College, Columbia University, 1932. Pp. x + 86.

HOPKINS, L. B. *Personnel Procedure in Education, The Educational Record.* Supplement, No. 3 (October, 1926). Washington: American Council on Education.

JONES, ARTHUR J. *Principles of Guidance.* New York: McGraw-Hill Co., 1930. Pp. xxiv + 385.

KATZ, DANIEL C. AND ALLPORT, FLOYD H. *Students' Attitudes.* Syracuse, N. Y.: The Craftsman Press, Inc., 1931. Pp. xxviii + 408.

KELLY, ROBERT LINCOLN. *Tendencies in College Administration.* Lancaster, Pa.: The Science Press, 1925. Pp. xii + 276.

LLOYD-JONES, ESTHER McD. *Student Personnel Work at Northwestern University.* New York: Harper & Brothers, 1929. Pp. xx + 253.

MATHIASEN, O. F. *Guidance and Placement in University Graduate Schools of Education.* Unpublished dissertation, Harvard University, 1927. Pp. 370.

MOFFETT, M'LEDGE. *The Social Background and Activities of Teachers College Students.* Contributions to Education, No. 375. New York: Bureau of Publications, Teachers College, Columbia University, 1929. Pp. vi + 133.

Research Bulletin of the National Education Association, Washington, D. C., VIII, 1 (January, 1930).

REYNOLDS, O. EDGAR. *Social and Economic Status of College Students.* Contributions to Education, No. 272. New York: Bureau of Publications, Teachers College, Columbia University, 1927. Pp. v + 57.

SMELTZER, C. H. "A Method for Determining What College Students Consider Their Own Difficulties." *School and Society,* XXXII, 709-710 (November 22, 1930).

SPENCE, RALPH B. "Factors Related to College Achievement." *Teachers College Record,* XXIX, 504-514 (March, 1928).

SPERLE, D. HENRYETTA. "Some Difficulties Experienced by First Year Students in Teacher Training Institutions." *Teachers College Record,* XXIX, 618-627 (April, 1928).

STRANG, RUTH M. "Personal Problems of Students." *Proceedings of the National Association of Deans of Women,* Washington, D. C.: Association, 1929.

SUZZALLO, HENRY. "The Use of Leisure." *Journal of the National Education Association.* XIX, 123-126 (April, 1930).

Appendices

APPENDIX A

STUDENT INQUIRY BLANK

Mr. Mrs. Miss_____

Local address_____ Telephone_____

Age: Under 25____; 25-34____; 35-44____; 45 and over____

Married_____ Single_____ Major subject_____

Are you working for a degree? Yes____ No____ Degree_____

Total number of points carried at Teachers College THIS SEMESTER_____

Total number of points carried elsewhere THIS SEMESTER _____

    TOTAL

Total number of points carried at Teachers College previously _____

Will you be willing to give thirty minutes of your time for an interview to discuss ways in which Teachers College may improve its personnel services to students?_____

If so, will you indicate at what hours you would be free for an interview, e.g. 10:30 Wednesday, Thursday, or Friday? _____ _____

Please think over carefully your most important personal problems *during your period of study at Teachers College.* This means those matters which have perplexed you most and for which you may or may not have found a satisfactory solution. They may be questions of leisure, finance, physical or mental health, emotional adjustments, social relationships, living conditions, vocational placement, home life, recreation, religion, part-time work; in short, any phase of your life. Then list below in the order of their importance to you your three major problems. PLEASE MAKE A SPECIAL EFFORT TO CHOOSE YOUR REALLY VITAL PROBLEMS.

Specific Problems e.g. Shall I carry full class schedule or work part-time?	Did You Consult Anyone Officially Connected with Teachers College?		Was Conference Helpful to You?		How Did You Solve the Problem?
	Yes or No	Whom?	Yes or No	If helpful, in what ways; if not, in what ways?	
1.					
2.					
3.					

Please think over carefully your most important problems *in connection with your academic work in Teachers College.* This includes many areas, such as: advisement, choice of major, use of the library, getting courses desired, determining requirements for degree, deciding whether to work toward a degree, maintaining satisfactory academic standing. PLEASE MAKE A SPECIAL EFFORT TO CHOOSE YOUR REALLY VITAL PROBLEMS AND TO STATE THEM SPECIFICALLY.

Problems	Did You Consult Anyone Officially Connected with Teachers College?		Was Conference Helpful to You?		How Did You Solve the Problem?
	Yes or No	Whom?	Yes or No	If helpful, in what ways; if not, in what ways?	
1.					
2.					
3.					

Note—If any of the above problems are peculiar to Summer Session, please star them.* PLEASE RETURN TO BOX 613 TEACHERS COLLEGE LOCAL POST OFFICE, MAIN HALL, T. C., AT YOUR EARLIEST CONVENIENCE. No Postage Required.

APPENDIX B

OUTLINE OF INTERVIEW WITH STUDENTS

Name____
Married____ Single____ Age____
New student____ Former student____
Full-time____ Part-time____ Number of points____
Degree____
Personal problems mentioned____
Academic problems mentioned____
Remarks:____

FINANCE

1. To what circumstances is your financial difficulty due?
    Unexpected expenses?____
    Living costs higher than anticipated?____
    Reduced income?____
    Loss of position?____
    Bank failure?____
    Inability to obtain part-time work?____
    Others____

2. How did you plan before you came to solve the problem?
   Borrow_____
   Part-time work_____
   Other ways_____
3. How are you solving it?
   Borrowing from college_____
   Borrowing from relatives and friends_____
   Borrowing from bank_____
   Working part-time_____
4. How much are you borrowing?_____ What interest do you pay?_____
5. Have you endeavored to get financial assistance from the college in the way of
   Scholarship?_____ Fellowship?_____ Loan?_____
6. Was the attempt successful?_____ If so, how much was received?_____
7. Are you dependent entirely on your own resources?_____
8. Are you responsible for the support of others?
   Father_____ Mother_____ Wife_____ Husband_____ Children
   _____ To what extent? Partially_____ Wholly_____
9. Would you have had a financial problem regardless of the present financial depression?_____

PLACEMENT

1. What is your specific problem in placement?_____
2. Have you had teaching experience?_____ How much?_____
3. Do you wish placement in the same type of work you were following before coming to Teachers College?_____
4. Are you majoring in this type of work at Teachers College?_____
5. If not, what change have you made?_____
6. Why?_____
7. If change in type of position is desired, wish to change from _____
   _____ to _____
8. Why?_____
9. Are you on leave of absence now?_____
10. If you left your previous position before coming to Teachers College, what was the reason for leaving:
    a. Reduction of expenses in school system?_____
    b. Work uncongenial?_____
    c. People uncongenial?_____
    d. Thought better position could be secured?_____
    e. _____
11. Have you consulted Bureau of Educational Service?_____
12. This fall?_____ Previously?_____ With what result?_____
13. Have you registered with outside agencies?_____
    With what result?_____
14. What other means have you used for obtaining a position?
    a. Application by letter_____
    b. Personal application_____
    c. Through efforts of friends_____
15. When do you desire placement? Now_____ Feb. 1932_____ Summer 1932_____ Fall 1932_____
16. Do you have in mind a particular position in which you desire placement?_____

PART-TIME WORK

1. Did you plan to do part-time work when you came to Teachers College?
   _____

2. Can you continue through the academic year without part-time work?
   _____

3. Is the problem that of:
   a. Obtaining part-time work?_____
   b. Present position not of type desired?_____
   c. Work interferes with class and study schedule?_____

4. If A
   a. How many times have you consulted Bureau of Part-Time Employment?_____
   b. How much work have you secured through the Bureau?_____
   c. Have you secured work through any other agency or person officially connected with Teachers College?_____ What agency?_____
   d. How much work have you secured through your friends?_____
   e. How much work have you secured through your own independent efforts?_____

5. If B
   a. What kind of work do you have now?_____
      How secured?_____
   b. Why is it objectionable?
      Small pay_____   Unpleasant in itself_____
      No educational value_____   Hours inconvenient_____

6. What kind of work do you want?_____

7. How many hours a week are you working?_____ How much are you paid per hour?_____ Per week?_____

8. At what hours do you work?_____

9. Does your work contribute to your professional advancement in any way?
   _____

10. What difficulties have you encountered in getting work?_____

11. Do you work part-time rather than borrow money because
    a. You are unable to borrow?_____
    b. Do not wish to go into debt?_____
    c. Other reasons_____

SOCIAL RELATIONSHIPS

1. Is the specific problem
   a. Lack of contacts with fellow students?_____
   b. Lack of contacts with people outside college?_____
   c. Lack of contacts with people own age?_____
   d. Lack of contacts with men?_____ Or women?_____
   e. Lack of contacts with interesting people?_____

2. Does the problem arise from:
   a. Lack of time for making social contacts?_____
   b. Lack of money for making contacts desired?_____
   c. 1. For clothes_____
      2. For dues_____
      3. For tickets_____
   d. Lack of ability to make social contacts?_____
   e. Lack of facilities for entertaining?
      1. No reception room_____
      2. Poor furnishings_____

    3. Inconvenient location_____
  f. Social direction?_____
    1. No opportunity to make acquaintances?_____
    2. Lack of interesting events?_____
3. What efforts have you made to solve the problem?
  a. Live in dormitory_____
  b. Live in International House_____
  c. Live in co-ed club_____
  d. Apartment_____
  e. Special efforts to be friendly_____
  f. _____
  g. _____
4. What difficulties have you encountered in trying to solve the problem?
5. Do you attend
  a. Graduate Club? All meetings_____ ¾_____ ½_____ ¼_____
    None_____
  b. Departmental Club? All meetings_____ ¾_____ ½_____
    ¼_____ None_____
  c. Educational Fraternities? All meetings_____ ¾_____ ½_____
    ¼_____ None_____
  d. Outside Organizations? All meetings_____ ¾_____ ½_____
    ¼_____ None_____
  e. Church? Every Sunday_____ Twice a month_____ Once a
    month_____ Less frequently_____
6. If none, why not?_____
7. What suggestions have you for improving the present situation?_____
_____

TIME DISTRIBUTION

1. Has problem arisen because
  a. You are working part-time?_____
  b. Keeping house for yourself?_____ Family?_____ How many?____
  c. Finding that your academic work requires more time than you were
    planning?_____
  d. Other causes_____
_____
2. Do you have a definite study and recreation schedule?_____
3. What difficulties have you encountered in trying to budget your time?
  a. Interruptions due to dormitory life_____
  b. Living with friends in apartment_____
  c. Unexpected assignments on part of professors_____
  d. _____

LIVING CONDITIONS

1. Where are you living at present?
  College (or University) hall? (name)_____
  Other hall or club (name)_____
  Apartment: Alone in apartment_____ Have room in large apartment
    _____ With husband_____ Wife_____ Children_____
    Parent_____ Others_____ With friend_____ Friends
    (No.)_____
  Room with family_____ Alone_____ With friend_____ Others
_____

2. Do your living arrangements offer special problems in regard to:
   Expense—Too expensive for means_____
   Too expensive for what is given_____
   Location—In relation to college_____
   In relation to street (noise_____) (dirt_____)
   In relation to sunlight_____
   In relation to other apartments or buildings_____
   In relation to bath and other facilities_____
   Size—In relation to cost_____
   In relation to comfort_____
   Furnishings—Incomplete_____
   Uncomfortable_____
   Service—Cleaning infrequent_____　Careless_____
   Elevator_____　Mail messages_____
   Regulations—Restrictions_____
   Opportunities for social life_____
3. What would you suggest in the way of improvements?
   (Would a coeducational hall offer a solution?_____)

ADVISEMENT

1. Is problem inability to obtain advisement
   a. From professors?_____
   b. From other officers?_____
   c. Information given inadequate?_____
   d. Information inaccurate?_____
   e. Conflicting advice?_____
   f. Not knowing whom to see for advice?_____
   g. Others_____
2. Is this a problem at
   a. Registration?_____
   b. Extending over full semester?_____
3. Did difficulty lie in
   a. Inability on your part to be here at times professors or other officers were free?_____
   b. Lack of time on part of professor or personnel officer?_____
   c. Lack of interest on part of professor or personnel officer?_____
   d. Inability to see person desired?_____
4. Did you wish advisement on
   a. Choice of courses?_____
   b. Whether to work for degree?_____
   c. Assistance in course?_____
   d. Others_____
5. Suggestions for improvement_____
   _____

CHOICE OF COURSES

1. What was the specific problem?
   a. Lack of knowledge of what courses to take to meet requirements for degree?_____
   b. Not knowing what courses you wanted to take?_____
   c. Others_____
2. What difficulties did you encounter trying to solve this?_____
   _____

3. Suggestions for solution of problem_____

CHOICE OF MAJOR

1. What was the specific problem?_____

2. What difficulty did you encounter in trying to solve it?_____

3. Suggestions for improvement_____

LIBRARY

1. Why was this a problem?
   a. Catalogue requirements not clear_____
   b. Inability to get information_____
   c. Information not clear_____
   d. Passed from one person to another_____
   e. Others_____
2. Is there a professor in your department to whom you feel free to go for advice?_____
3. Would you like to have some one professor who would share with you the responsibility of working out your program; in other words, would a definitely appointed adviser be desirable?_____

WHETHER TO WORK FOR A DEGREE

1. Why was_____, or is_____, this a problem?
   a. Lack of funds to continue for degree_____
   b. Undecided about major field_____
   c. Undecided whether degree is worth money and effort required_____
   d. Too much strain on physical health_____
   e. Would mean carrying part-time_____ full-time_____ job at same time.
   f. Question of your own ability_____
2. What have you done about it?_____

APPENDIX C

INTERVIEW CARD USED BY PERSONNEL OFFICERS AND PROFESSORS

Office_____   Mr._____

Interviewer_____   Name: Miss_____

Date: Mrs._____

Voluntary_____ Requested_____ Age: 20–25, 25–35, 35–45, 45–55, over 55

Referred by_____

Initial Interview_____ Candidate for: B.S._____ M.A._____ Ph.D._____

Statement of Problem:

Satisfactory solution_____ (state solution briefly on back of card)
No satisfactory solution_____
Problem referred to_____
Time in minutes_____

APPENDIX D

DAILY TIME SCHEDULE

Name _____

	MONDAY	TUESDAY	WEDNESDAY	THURSDAY	FRIDAY	SATURDAY	SUNDAY
7:45–8	dress	dress	dress	dress	dress		
8– 9	travel; correct papers	travel; correct papers				dress	
9–10	Amtorg class	Amtorg class	Amtorg class	Amtorg class	Amtorg class		dress
10–11	travel; read newspaper	travel; prepare lesson A.	travel; read newspaper	travel; prepare lesson A.	travel; read newspaper	class psychology	breakfast;
11–12	class psychology	prepare outline on	class psychology	Macmillan's re easy reading	class Gates		professional guests; discuss education
12– 1	library on statistics; eat	phonetics	study statistics	material; eat	study Holling		in Arabia
1– 2	class statistics	eat; travel	class statistics		class statistics	lunch	read four books
2– 3	conference re this chart		eat		eat		
3– 4	library on statistics and phonetics	dentist	interview people	classify words for vocabulary tests		study psychology	teaching English to
4– 5	[travel; make lesson plan with		wanting to work for me		read for Cram group		foreigners
5– 6	[my sec. Amtorg laboratory period	see about pictures for phonetics;	conference on				
6– 7	travel	took trial snaps; eat	phonetics for City College				supper
7– 8	guest out of town; class		dinner	travel; class		read psychology for	
8– 9	read for	City College	date	City College	prelim. Cram	Cram group	guests
9–10	research on phonetics	travel	theatre	look up references on l. learning			read Gates
10–11	bed	date		Psy. Abst. and outline	travel home		Ed. Psy.
11–12			make lesson plans	bed	undress chat	bed	bed
12– 7		1 P.M. bed	bed		bed		